GETTING INTO THE ZONES OF REGULATION™

The Complete Framework and Digital Curriculum Companion

LEAH M. KUYPERS, MA ED. OTR/L

Think Social Publishing, Inc. Santa Clara, CA
www.socialthinking.com

**Getting Into The Zones of Regulation™:
The Complete Framework and Digital Curriculum Companion**
Written and created by Leah M. Kuypers, MA Ed. OTR/L
www.zonesofregulation.com

Copyright © 2024 The Zones of Regulation, Inc.

Published by Think Social Publishing, Inc.
404 Saratoga Avenue, Suite 200
Santa Clara, CA 95050
Tel: (408) 557-8595

All rights reserved except as noted herein.

Outside of the specific use described below, all other reproduction/copying, adaptation, conversion to electronic format, or sharing/distribution of content, through print or electronic means, is not permitted without written permission from The Zones of Regulation, Inc.

This includes prohibition of any use of any content or materials from this product as part of an adaptation or derivative work you create for posting on a personal or business website, TeachersPayTeachers, YouTube, Pinterest, Facebook, or any other social media or information-sharing site in existence now or in the future, whether free or for a fee. Exceptions are made, upon written request, for product reviews, articles, research and blogposts.

The Zones of Regulation, Inc. grants permission to the owner of this book to use and/or adapt content in print or electronic form, **only** for direct in-classroom/school/home or in-clinic use with your own students/clients/children, and includes parents/caregivers and direct service personnel. The copyright for any adaptation of content owned by The Zones of Regulation, Inc. remains with The Zones of Regulation, Inc. as a derivative work.

Social Thinking, Superflex, The UnthinkaBots, The Unthinkables, The Thinkables, and We Thinkers! GPS are trademarks belonging to Think Social Publishing, Inc. (TSP). The Zones of Regulation is a trademark belonging to Leah Kuypers, a TSP author.

Translation of this product can only be done in accordance with TSP's TRANSLATION POLICY found on our intellectual property website page here: https://www.socialthinking.com/intellectual-property. And, visit our intellectual property page to find detailed TERMS OF USE information and a DECISION-TREE that cover copyright, trademark, and intellectual property topics and questions governing the use of our materials.

ISBN: 978-1-962301-03-9

Book design by Sandra Salamony Editorial Design in collaboration with
The Zones of Regulation, Inc.

Emotion illustrations by Giovanni Abeille.

This book was printed and bound in the United States by Mighty Color Printing.

TSP is a sole source provider of Social Thinking products in the United States.

Books may be purchased online at www.socialthinking.com.

TO DANIEL AND VIVIAN,
MY GREATEST TEACHERS,
YOU ARE EVERYTHING.

CONTENTS

PREFACE x
    Reflections from the Author x
    What's New to The Zones of Regulation? xiv
        Getting Into The Zones xiv
        The Zones of Regulation® Digital Curriculum xv
    Acknowledgments xvi

CHAPTER 1: REGULATION FROM THE INSIDE OUT

OVERVIEW AND GOALS 1
WHAT IS REGULATION? 2
    Self-regulation and Co-regulation 3
    Expect Dysregulation 4
WHY DOES REGULATION MATTER? 4
    Regulation and Social Emotional Learning (SEL) 5
BEYOND BEHAVIOR: UNDERSTANDING
THE UNDERLYING FACTORS IMPACTING REGULATION 6
    What's Under the Hood: Neurobiological
    Considerations Impacting Regulation 7
        Developmental Nature of Regulation Strategies 9
        Sensory Processing and Interoception 11
        Executive Functioning 14
        Emotional Regulation 15
        Social Cognition 17
        Context and Prediction 19
        Trauma and the Nervous System 20
    What's the Terrain: The Impact of Lived Experience on Regulation . . 22
        Relationships 23
        Culture 24
        Sociopolitical Environment 25
        Experience with Disciplinary Measures 25
        Access to Supports 27
CONCLUSION 28
    Apply Your Learning 28
        Reflection Question 28
        Pair & Share with a Colleague 29
LEADER REFLECTION ACTIVITY: Factors Impacting Regulation xiv

CHAPTER 2: WHAT IS THE ZONES OF REGULATION?

OVERVIEW AND GOALS 31
WHAT IS THE ZONES OF REGULATION? 32

v

CONTENTS

CATEGORIZING FEELINGS INTO THE ZONES: SIGNATURE PRACTICE 1 33
    Learners: Who Can Benefit? 33
    Leaders: Who Can Teach? 33
    Why Use Colors to Teach about Regulation? 34
    The Neuroscience Behind The Zones 35

THE FOUR ZONES SENSATIONS AND SIGNALS 36
    Blue Zone 37
    Green Zone 37
    Yellow Zone 38
    Red Zone 39
    All The Zones Are Okay 40

OFFER ZONES CHECK-INS: SIGNATURE PRACTICE 2 41
    Check-In Benefits for Learners 41
    Check-In Benefits for Leaders 41

REGULATING OUR ZONES WITH TOOLS 42
    Regulating the Blue Zone 43
    Regulating the Green Zone 43
    Regulating the Yellow Zone 44
    Regulating the Red Zone 44

CREATE CUSTOM ZONES TOOLBOXES: SIGNATURE PRACTICE 3 ... 45
    Tool Tips 45

USE THE ZONES PATHWAY: SIGNATURE PRACTICE 4 46
    Pathway Variables 47
    The Zones Pathway in Action 48
        Step 1: Notice 48
        Step 2: Check-in 48
        Step 3: Decide 48
        Step 4: Regulate 49
        Step 5: Reflect 49

KEY PRINCIPLES OF THE ZONES OF REGULATION 50
CONCLUSION 51
    Apply Your Learning 52
        Reflection Questions 52
        Pair & Share with a Colleague 53
LEADER REFLECTION ACTIVITY: My Zones and Signals 54
LEADER REFLECTION ACTIVITY: My Zones Pathway Reflection . 55

CHAPTER 3: BUILDING THE ZONES CLIMATE

OVERVIEW AND GOALS 57
BENEFITS OF THE ZONES CLIMATE 58
BUILDING THE FOUNDATION FOR REGULATION: TAKING ACTION .. 59
    1. Regulate Yourself 59
    2. Build Relationships 61
    3. Co-regulate with Learners 63
    4. Cultivate Inclusion 64
    5. Make Sense of Behavior 66

CONTENTS

ESSENTIAL ELEMENTS FOR A ZONES CLIMATE 68
    The Zones Climate Classroom Vignette 68
    Element 1: Provide Direct Instruction and Practice Opportunities 71
    Element 2: Post Zones Visuals 71
    Element 3: Offer Zones Check-Ins 74
    Element 4: Easy Access to Regulation Tools 75
    Element 5: Use Zones Language 78
        Own Your Zone 79

RESPONDING TO BEHAVIOR IN THE MOMENT 80
    Restorative Practices 81

CONTEXT AND CLIMATE IMPACTING THE ZONES PATHWAY 82

ZONES CLIMATE ASSESSMENT TOOLS 82

CONCLUSION 84
    Apply Your Learning 84
        Reflection Questions 84
        Pair & Share with a Colleague 85

LEADER REFLECTION ACTIVITY: Building the Foundation for Regulation:
My Actions 86

LEADER REFLECTION ACTIVITY: Identifying The Zones Climate Practices 87

CHAPTER 4: TEACHING THE ZONES OF REGULATION CURRICULUM

OVERVIEW AND GOALS 89

INTRODUCTION TO *THE ZONES OF REGULATION® DIGITAL CURRICULUM* 90
    Scope and Sequence 90
    Concept Components 91
        Universal Design for Learning (UDL) 94

CONCEPT GUIDE PREVIEW 95

HOW TO IMPLEMENT THE ZONES CURRICULUM 98
    Instruction Guidelines 98
    Pacing Each Concept (Concept Instruction Plan) 99
        Recommendations for Concept Pacing 100
    Pacing the Curriculum 100
    Spiraling Instruction 101
        Spiraling Within the Instructional Period 101
        Spiraling Over the Years 101

HOW TO TEACH A CONCEPT 103
    Concept Prep Checklist 103
    Using the Interactive Presentation 103
        Recommendations for Engaging Learners
        Throughout an Interactive Presentation 104
    Differentiate with Geared Activities 105
        Deciding Which Geared Activity Is Right for Your Learners 105

AN OVERVIEW OF GEARED ACTIVITIES 106
    Adapt for Learners 107
        Considerations 107
        Zones in Individualized Learning Plans 108
        Overlaying The Zones with Other SEL Resources 109

CONTENTS

    Extend Learning 109
        The Zones Climate 109
        Bridging The Zones: Connect with Supportive Adults 110
        More Zones Resources 110
WAYS TO CHECK FOR LEARNING AND MEASURE PROGRESS 112
    Observation and Questioning: What to Watch For 113
        Learner Assessment Tools 114
        Zones Climate and Implementation Assessment Tools 115
    Check for Learning 115
    Learner Self-monitoring 115
IMPLEMENT THE ZONES IN DIFFERENT SETTINGS 115
    Roles to Support Implementation 116
    Home 116
    What Can The Zones Look Like in Different Settings? 117
    Schools and Classrooms 118
        The Zones Across Tiered Instruction 118
        Connect to Academic Standards 120
        Schoolwide Implementation 121
CONCLUSION 122
    Apply Your Learning 123
        Get Started! 123
LEADER REFLECTION ACTIVITY: Concept Planner: Concept 1 124
LEADER REFLECTION ACTIVITY: Foundational Planning 125

APPENDIX 126
    Chapter 1
        Sensory Preferences and Lifestyle 127
        Tools for Assessing Regulation Competencies 128
        Zones of Regulation Digital Curriculum
        and CASEL Competency Correlation Chart 130
    Chapter 3
        Zones Check-In Considerations 131
        Zones Language 132
        The Zones Climate Rubric 133
    Chapter 4
        Concept Planner 137
        Sample Individualized Regulation Goals 138
        Zones in the Home 139
        MTSS/PBIS and Zones of Regulation Crosswalk 140
        Regulation Self-reflection 141
        Learning Target Rubric 143
        Observing Regulation Competencies 146
        Digital Curriculum Implementation and Fidelity Checklist . . . 148
ABOUT THE AUTHOR 154

CONTENTS

LEADER RESOURCES
(See the last page of the book for download link.)

Chapter 1
Leader Reflection Activity: Factors Impacting Regulation 2
Sensory Preferences and Lifestyle 3
Zones of Regulation Digital Curriculum
  and CASEL Competency Correlation Chart 4

Chapter 2
Leader Reflection Activity: My Zones and Signals 5
Leader Reflection Activity: My Zones Pathway Reflection 6

Chapter 3
Zones Check-In Considerations 7
Zones Language 8
The Zones Climate Rubric 9
Leader Reflection Activity: Building the Foundation for Regulation: My Actions . . . 13
Leader Reflection Activity: Identifying Zones Climate Practices 14

Chapter 4
Concept Planner 15
Sample Individualized Regulation Goals 16
Zones in the Home 17
MTSS/PBIS and Zones of Regulation Crosswalk 18
Leader Reflection Activity: Foundational Planning 19
Regulation Self-reflection 20
Learning Target Rubric 22
Observing Regulation Competencies 25
Leader Reflection Activity: Concept Planner: Concept 1 26
Digital Curriculum Implementation and Fidelity Checklist 27

Online Bibliography and Resources
(Visit www.socialthinking.com/getting-into-the-zones to locate the listing.)

IX

PREFACE

The Zones of Regulation, Inc. Mission Statement

We believe that regulation is essential for leading a healthy and meaningful life. The Zones of Regulation empowers learners of all ages to understand the full range of their feelings, as well as explore tools and strategies to support their well-being.

REFLECTIONS FROM THE AUTHOR

Before I present the latest theory regarding The Zones of Regulation framework, I'd like to reflect on the origins of The Zones and its evolution since 2011

I conceived The Zones of Regulation when I was working in public schools as an occupational therapist (OT) and autism resource specialist. I encountered learners of all ages, with all types of needs. I was struck by how often their challenges in regulation skills impacted their adaptive functioning and sense of well-being in the home, school, and community. Whatever their diagnosis or educational label, these challenges might be perceived as a learner appearing silly and losing a sense of control, becoming distracted and missing pertinent information, shutting down, exploding, or acting out aggressively.

These behaviors hurt the learners. Time was taken away from learning and they strained social relations with peers and staff. Sometimes even punitive measures were taken in response, like restraints, suspensions, and/or exclusion. The results were unfair and unacceptable.

As the OT, I worked with learners to address sensory regulation differences. However, no matter what treatment I provided, differences in the learners' emotional regulation, social cognition, executive functioning, and impulse control continued to stand in the way of their successes. I realized we needed to examine the larger picture of regulation: its relationship to other social and emotional differences and challenges these learners had experienced. We also needed to change the culture in which the behavior was viewed and addressed.

I saw too that many of the methods being used—such as point sheets, level systems, and time-outs—to curb what others perceived as undesired behavior, didn't address the core issue of developing underlying skills. Trying to modify behaviors based on rewards and punishments doesn't work, and research supports this observation. In writing about promising school-based interventions for reducing aggressive behavior, Riccomini, Zhang, and Katsiyannis (2005) report that exclusions are found to be counterproductive in reducing negative behavior and are connected to increased rates of grade detention, school dropout, academic failure, and delinquency.

The solution was clear to me. Learners of all ages needed to be taught regulation competencies aligned to their developmental continuum and be given opportunities to practice the skills in a safe and supportive environment. Inspired by Kari Dunn Buron's and Mitzi Curtis's *The Incredible 5-Point Scale* (2003), I developed an approach to address regulation in a systematic and pragmatic way as I completed a Graduate Certificate in Autism. I named this approach "The Zones of Regulation" or "The Zones" for short.

I taught the concept of The Zones of Regulation during my occupational therapy sessions and social learning groups in schools and saw encouraging results:

- Braden, who had a full-time educational assistant assigned to him in first grade, was able to move on to second grade without any aide support.

- Leo told me that he finally had a way to make sense of his feelings and knew how to deal with them. His teacher noticed too, giving him his first "E"s for excellence in areas such as "self-control" and "personal decision-making."

- Jayla used to frequently run out of the building. Now she tells staff through Zones Visuals how she is feeling, and the staff respects her need to move to a quiet, safe place designated for her within the school.

Many learners—as they gained abilities to recognize and communicate their feelings and use their Zones tools to regulate—significantly cut down their time spent outside the classroom in restraints and seclusion.

PREFACE

I decided (after much encouragement from my colleagues) to develop and organize The Zones into a curriculum that could reach a greater number of learners. The curriculum was first written as a capstone, to fulfill my Master of Arts in Education degree under the guidance of Kari Dunn Buron, who served on my capstone committee. Shortly afterward, *The Zones of Regulation*™ was published in 2011 by Think Social Publishing, Inc. (TSP, also known as "Social Thinking"). Michelle Garcia Winner, founder of the Social Thinking® Methodology, helped focus and strengthen the curriculum.

I am grateful to have the advice and support of esteemed authors, amazing colleagues, and inspired users around the globe who have helped shape The Zones into what it has become. As I continued to use The Zones with learners and provided training around the world to thousands of people, it became increasingly clear that an update was needed. I was evolving The Zones concepts and wanted to share them as well as clarify content that I was seeing misused. I proposed updating *The Zones of Regulation* in 2015 but, as the saying goes, there's a time and place for everything—2015 was not my time.

Shortly after meeting with my publisher, I had to put my work on hold to focus on another, more important job: helping my son with his health and regulation needs. In the fall of 2015, my son got sick. He developed pediatric acute neuropsychiatric syndrome (PANS) after a bout of pneumonia along with several other medical conditions. Our family was turned upside down.

I found myself living and breathing a new life as a distraught, barely functioning parent trying to support a suddenly highly dysregulated 5-year-old child amid a medical and mental health crisis—while also caring for a 2-year-old. I now had the perspective of a parent desperate to help a child who, despite my and my husband's best efforts and expertise, was still falling apart.

As my son got better with time and medical and therapeutic interventions, I took on collaborative writing projects building on The Zones of Regulation with dear friends and close colleagues, Elizabeth Sautter and Terri Rossman. Together we authored the *Navigating The Zones* board game (TSP, 2018) and the accompanying *Advanced Pack* (TSP, 2018). Elizabeth and I went on to write *The Zones of Regulation Storybook Set* (TSP, 2021) and create the *Tools to Try Cards for Kids* (TSP, 2020) and *Tools to Try Cards for Tweens & Teens* (TSP, 2021). (See page 42 for more information on these products.)

Through the development of these new products and creative endeavors, The Zones of Regulation framework evolved into a concrete way to teach regulation as a cognitive pathway or mental roadmap. I consulted and collaborated with parents, teachers, and practitioners of all disciplines. They encouraged me to think about how to adapt The Zones for different audiences—early childhood, tweens/teens, and adult learners—and how to integrate it with other approaches including trauma-informed and culturally responsive teaching.

During these years the book's popularity soared. More classrooms, schools, and districts around the world adopted The Zones as common practice, leading to valuable insights on how to extend the framework into Tier 1 (whole class/whole school) instruction so all learners can benefit. And my organization expanded to support this growth. First my sister, Molly Schock, joined me as my Director of Operations, helping evolve the training to include a webinar format to meet the needs of an expanding Zones audience. Then Emily Walz came on as the Director of Instruction, helping me create valuable new Zones educational content, including being a critical thought partner in the development of *The Zones of Regulation Digital Curriculum*. She brought new light to different applications of the framework and has been essential in evolving conversations around race, equity, and schoolwide implementation.

Then along comes the COVID-19 pandemic, forcing me to think creatively on how to deliver instruction virtually to learners at home. More than ever, we had to support caregivers by making learning content accessible and easy to integrate into the home.

The killing of George Floyd and the events surrounding his death also deeply affected me, my home city of Minneapolis, and the world. It encouraged me to learn how to become a stronger advocate and ally for our BIPOC (Black, Indigenous, and People of Color) community. Also, listening to the neurodivergent voices—as well as following the neurodiversity paradigm shift—has been eye-opening and pertinent to my work. These events showed me that my best intentions aren't always good enough and I needed to update the language, visuals, scope, and accessibility of *The Zones of Regulation*™.

As I listened to our audience, I heard over and over the call for more digital access to the Zones content. Knowing that there were profound shifts in the delivery of educational content as a result of the pandemic, it became increasingly clear that the next iteration of The Zones of Regulation must have a digital component. Looking forward, I also set three big goals:

1. Improve content accessibility and engagement for learners.

2. Increase ease of implementation for leaders (or facilitators).

PREFACE

3. Increase fidelity and leader confidence by making what must be taught more explicit and user-friendly.

I continued to expand my Zones family to include Adam Berkin, our Director of Education, and Stephen Perepeluk, our Head of Strategic Initiatives, to help me meet the goals I laid out. What has resulted is two things, the first is this *Getting Into The Zones of Regulation™: The Complete Framework and Digital Curriculum Companion* guide. The second, a companion to this guide, is an all-new *[The] Zones of Regulation® Digital Curriculum*. Although the new theory and updates around The Zones did not arrive on the timeline I originally hoped or intended, I've learned to trust the process and now believe everything happens for a reason. I'm grateful for the enriching experiences (albeit some unwelcome ones) gained these 14 years that informed my work and transformed its evolution.

To read more about the story behind The Zones, please visit www.zonesofregulation.com.

> **NOTE TO READER:** In both *Getting Into The Zones* and *The Zones Digital Curriculum,* I use the word learner rather than student, child, etc., because people of all ages can benefit from learning regulation competencies. I refer to the facilitator or teacher as the leader. I also use identity-first language to honor the identity of individuals and mean no disrespect to those who prefer person-first language.

WHAT'S NEW TO THE ZONES OF REGULATION?

Getting Into The Zones

Getting Into The Zones sets you up to be successful in understanding and applying The Zones of Regulation framework. One of the important lessons I have learned over the years is that learning begins with us, the adults in our youths' lives. We need to first examine and widen our lens and practices around regulation before teaching regulation to our learners. In *Getting Into The Zones*, we will explore the many facets of regulation so we can better understand our learners and how best to help them. This understanding is vital whether you go on to implement *The Zones of Regulation Digital Curriculum* or not. In addition, you will also find the following new topics:

- Defining regulation and why it matters
- Regulation and social emotional learning (SEL)
- Development of regulation strategies
- Neurobiological considerations impacting regulation
- The impact of lived experiences on regulation
- ACEs/Trauma-informed care considerations

- Neurodiversity-affirming practices
- Culturally responsive teaching strategies
- Using a structured system for regulation
- Key tenets of The Zones of Regulation
- The Zones of Regulation Pathway
- How to create a Zones Climate
- Zones alignment to CASEL competencies
- Zones instructional models, scope, and sequence
- Adult social emotional learning (SEL) woven throughout

After reading this book, you will have all the knowledge and understanding I've gained from the last decade-plus of supporting regulation using The Zones of Regulation, and therefore I feel confident you will have what you need to implement the *The Zones Digital Curriculum* (see below) as it is intended.

The Zones of Regulation® Digital Curriculum

The Zones of Regulation Digital Curriculum (sold separately via subscription at www.zonesofregulation.com) equips you with the resources to teach The Zones of Regulation framework. The new digital curriculum is informed by my work with learners, schools, families, practitioners, and community partners over the years. The lesson concepts include the best from the original curriculum, along with numerous enhancements to make implementation easier for you, as well as more engaging for your learners. Each lesson concept includes the following:

- Ready-to-use digital presentations with interactive activities and videos to engage learners.

- Integration of Universal Design for Learning (UDL) to minimize barriers for learners of different ages and abilities. This includes numerous extension activities geared for instruction at different ages and support levels.

- A guide with detailed step-by-step teaching points and suggestions for differentiating and extending learning.

- Easy access to downloadable resources:
  - Updated graphics, visual supports, and activity sheets
  - Formative assessments
  - School-to-home connection (the Bridge)

The Zones of Regulation Digital Curriculum also includes the following new Zones of Regulation core Concepts:

PREFACE

- What Is Regulation?
- Introducing The Zones of Regulation
- All The Zones Are Okay
- My Signals, My Zones
- The Zones Check-In
- Situations that Trigger and Spark
- What Is a Regulation Tool?
- Building My Zones Toolbox
- Deciding to Regulate
- The Zones Pathway

DISCLAIMER: The information contained in this book is for informational purposes only and is not to be used for the purposes of diagnosing or treating mental or physical health conditions. Consult your health care provider for any concerns you may have.

All stories and names used within the book have been altered to protect the identity of individuals. They are composites of real situations within educational settings.

ACKNOWLEDGMENTS FOR GETTING INTO THE ZONES AND THE ZONES OF REGULATION DIGITAL CURRICULUM

First and foremost, I'd like to thank Emily Walz: I could not have done this without you. You are the ultimate thought partner, and your input enriched this content exponentially. You helped me over the hump so many times and kept me focused on my goals when I was pulled in so many directions. You carried the torch and charged ahead with development of the *Digital Curriculum* too many times to count.

Adam Berkin, you believed in me and gave me the confidence to make my own destiny. *Getting Into The Zones of Regulation* and the *Digital Curriculum* would not have come together so beautifully without your hands-on input and coordination.

Molly Schock, not only are you an amazing sister, but your equally amazing talent to keep The Zones of Regulation, Inc. running smoothly gave me the space to write, create, and further develop The Zones framework and content.

Hannah Money, your design and intuition for transforming ideas into accessible, informative, and appealing visuals, videos, handouts,

PREFACE

and slides were invaluable. You have made The Zones sparkle, and it is such a pleasure to work alongside my cousin.

Stephen Perepeluk and David Stirling, I painted a vision for you and you built it in rapid time. Thank you for taking these big ideas of mine and making them a reality with the digital platform.

Elizabeth Sautter, you have been my number-one cheerleader since the day I met you and plopped that binder of an unpublished draft of The Zones of Regulation curriculum on that restaurant table. You have helped me dream big, push my thinking, build my business as well as being a partner in projects, listening to my woes, and being one amazing friend along the way. Thank you for your contributions!

To the team at Social Thinking—Michelle Garcia Winner, Mary Ann Hall, Pam Crooke, Sarah Halicki—thank you for all your feedback, edits, and efforts to shape this content into a book.

I'd also like to thank Hannah Radiant and Endurance Learning, and the team at Magic Box, for all the education technology expertise you brought to this project to transform lessons into a digital medium on a digital platform.

Thank you to the expert readers and consultants who provided feedback along the way, including Luis Perez and Allison Posey at CAST, the team at the Innocent Classroom, Katie Pagnotta, Sarah Ann Lentz, a neurodivergent reader, and Ruth Prystash. I appreciate your edits and input.

Thank you St. Paul Public Schools and Annie Goerdt and the CAREI team at the University of Minnesota for partnering in research on the *Digital Curriculum* to guide its development.

Lastly, a huge thanks goes out to my family. Vivian and Daniel, your encouragement and patience, along with your feedback and involvement, are things I am so grateful for. David, the countless hours you spent editing everything have been vital to production, but you have also been my person to lean on and steady me. I love you.

CHAPTER 1
REGULATION FROM THE INSIDE OUT

OVERVIEW AND GOALS

In this chapter, I'm going to break down some of the core neurobiological components that play a role in regulation. I'll describe how lived experiences (e.g., sociopolitical factors, access, and relationships) can impact a person's ability to regulate. Appreciating how all these factors intersect can help us gain a deeper understanding of our learners, and in turn guide our instruction to be more compassionate and caring. To ensure The Zones of Regulation is used in the way it was intended, as a learner-focused framework, we must begin with understanding regulation and **our role** as leaders (or facilitators) in helping it flourish.

Working in schools, clinics, and homes, I've found that it's easy for adults to become focused on learners' negative behaviors. They mistakenly blame learners, their families, or even cultures for differences and difficulties learners have around regulation. This deficit-based thinking is harmful because it doesn't allow for the pure innocence of the learner to be seen, acknowledged, and valued, nor for their strengths to be built upon. It also doesn't account for the underlying factors that may be impacting regulation. This mindset impedes the expectations adults set for a learner.

A different approach is needed. We know that a major component of success and well-being in school, home, and community is the ability to regulate our feelings and responses as best we can when we are stressed. With The Zones of Regulation, I set out to do better for all learners and provide the adults with the tools to support and teach

> **GOALS FOR CHAPTER**
>
> - Understand the competency of regulation, including underlying neurobiological components and external contributing factors.
>
> - Shift the lens of leaders to establish a compassionate mindset and approach with all learners in how we view behavior and support regulation.

CHAPTER 1: Regulation from the Inside Out

COMPETENCY: A combination of one's knowledge, skills, and behaviors that leads to being successful at something. Competencies can be used across a range of experiences.

SKILL: A proficiency or strength gained via experience or training.

these competencies. It is vital that adults understand the nature of regulation. I liken this to teaching literacy; I wouldn't walk into a first-grade classroom and start teaching kids how to read without training in the foundations of teaching reading. The same goes for regulation. Without this underlying information, all too often a learner's lack of regulation skills gets overlooked as challenging behavior, and curbing that behavior becomes the focus of intervention.

WHAT IS REGULATION?

Most simply defined, **regulation** is to adjust, manage, or control something so it works well. When applied to humans, regulation can go by many names, such as "self-control," "self-management," "emotional control," "anger management," or "impulse control." These terms all describe a person's ability to adjust their state of alertness, energy level, and emotions to help them attain personal goals, meet the demands of the situation around them, and gain a sense of well-being. Physiologically, when we are regulated, our brain and body, integrated via the nervous system, work together to manage the situation at hand. Being regulated can play out in many

Connecting to The Zones of Regulation

Throughout this chapter, and in Chapter 4, look for the boxes with this icon to see how the concepts you are reading about are integrated in *The Zones of Regulation® Digital Curriculum.*

Inspired by my caseload, I developed The Zones of Regulation to help learners of all ages develop and refine their competency in regulation. In The Zones, we shift the lens from deficit-based thinking toward focusing on a strength-based, skill development mindset. In this way we honor each learner's abilities, competencies, and strengths and focus on opportunities and possibilities for growth. The Zones of Regulation also helps solve the problem of behaviorally based interventions, which have been shown to be ineffective and even harmful. We've pioneered an alternative approach to practices that haven't served learners or acknowledged their authentic experiences.

The Zones of Regulation is a unique and systematic approach to help unpack some of the complexity of regulation and build the capacity to recognize when we're in different physiological and emotional states, as well as pair tools that support regulation of that state. We call these states "The Zones," with each of the zones represented by a distinct color. We categorize all the different ways we feel—including our feelings, energy levels, and states of alertness—into four colored zones. Using the four Zones, we can establish an easy language with visual supports and structure that not only help build competencies to self-regulate but also co-regulate with others.

ways, such as asking for help when you're feeling stressed from a writing assignment, using journaling to help you cope when you're feeling down and distraught, or revving yourself up to play in a football game when your energy is low by doing a quick set of jumping jacks. We regulate all the following processes: sensory input and needs, internal nervous system states, emotions, energy levels, and impulses.

Dysregulation is the opposite of regulation and describes the imbalance in our internal state, such as when we physiologically feel "off" or are experiencing sensory overload in a busy environment. In addition, dysregulation can be used to describe our emotions and behavior, such as when we aren't able to manage our feelings and react with behavior that doesn't serve us well. When we are dysregulated, our nervous system is often flooded with stress hormones that affect our brain and body and interfere with our well-being.

SELF-REGULATION AND CO-REGULATION

We can regulate in one of two ways: self-regulation or co-regulation. **Self-regulation** is independently managing feelings and states to attain goals (whether personal, social, or academic/professional) to meet the demands of our situation and support a sense of well-being. **Co-regulation** is the process of connecting, or being attuned, with a social partner for support in attaining goals, meeting demands, and finding a sense of well-being. Co-regulation is something we can both provide as well as receive. To understand the difference, let's consider the following example:

A learner in the classroom is feeling frustrated trying to solve a math equation.

- **Self-regulation:** Arjun independently works through his feelings of frustration and finds a strategy (commonly referred to as "regulation tool") that allows him to complete the equation. He uses positive self-talk (such as saying to himself, "I can do this," or "I'm going to take some deep breaths and try again") to guide him through the feelings and become able to refocus.

- **Co-regulation:** Daniella raises her hand and, with a heavy sigh, shares her frustration with her teacher, "I don't get this." The teacher, attuned to Daniella's feelings, supports her well-being by offering encouragement and providing further teaching to help clear up any confusion.

As our metacognitive thinking skills develop, we become more skilled at self-regulation, but even as adults we co-regulate. Have you ever

REGULATION is to adjust, manage, or control something so it works well.

DYSREGULATION is the opposite of regulation and describes the imbalance in our internal state, such as when we physiologically feel "off" or are experiencing sensory overload in a busy environment.

SELF-REGULATION is independently managing feelings and states to attain goals (whether personal, social, or academic/professional) to meet the demands of our situation and support a sense of well-being.

CO-REGULATION is the process of connecting, or being attuned, with a social partner for support in attaining goals, meeting demands, and finding a sense of well-being.

NOTE: The broader term "regulate/regulation," (rather than self- or co-regulate/regulation) will most often be referenced through this book and the curriculum given it captures the fluidity between the two.

CHAPTER 1: Regulation from the Inside Out

Zones Connection: Fostering Regulation

In *The Zones of Regulation Digital Curriculum,* you'll learn how to foster competencies in self-regulation for your learners while concurrently serving as a co-regulator for them during the ups and downs of their day as they are building skills.

vented to a colleague about a work situation that is frustrating you or leaned on a loved one for a hug and pep talk when you're feeling sad? We *all* need co-regulation with and from others for support.

EXPECT DYSREGULATION

As we build regulation competencies within ourselves and our learners, it's important to keep in mind that no one regulates perfectly. All of us, from adults with years of experience regulating to preschoolers who are just learning to put language to feelings, will inevitably have times when we struggle to regulate. For example, who hasn't stayed up way too late watching a movie when you know you need to wake up early, had your anxiety and/or stress impact your productivity at work by ruminating on a problem, or sent an email in the heat of the moment instead of waiting to push "send." Dysregulation is a fact of life, and we can all expect it to happen.

Part of growing our capacity to regulate is finding ways to move on when we don't regulate well and regret our behavior. Moving on might look like:

- Taking responsibility.
- Forgiving oneself (we all make mistakes).
- Repairing or restoring relationships.
- Planning for next time, which can involve asking for help.

As we build our emotional awareness and regulation skills, we gain a deeper understanding of what is happening in the moments when our regulation is not quite working for us. This awareness helps us grow in our regulation, and move on with more ease. Make sure to give yourself grace, as well as your learners, when dysregulation occurs—it is expected!

WHY DOES REGULATION MATTER?

Working in schools, I saw a clear divide. Individuals who could regulate with ease more likely received an inclusive education, enjoyed social circles, had positive rapport with staff, and had better self-esteem. But others struggled to regulate their feelings, sensory needs, and behaviors which resulted in missed educational opportunities, strained peer relationships, poor rapport with staff, and feelings of shame and loneliness.

Your ability to regulate your emotional, physical, and energetic state is critical for being able to work toward personal goals. Regulation is key to having fun, completing tasks, working effectively on a team, maintaining healthy and meaningful relationships, achieving academically and in your career, navigating the community, and having an overall sense of well-being. It plays a huge role in finding success in school and in life.

REGULATION AND SOCIAL EMOTIONAL LEARNING (SEL)

There's an ever-increasing body of research around social emotional learning (SEL) programs that includes regulation competencies that show their importance in life for all learners. A strong base of research indicates the correlation between SEL opportunities and instruction with overall positive outcomes for children and youth in terms of their engagement, mental health, academic functioning and achievement, self-efficacy, and reduced negative behavioral interactions—in addition to positive future benefits into adulthood.

In the 2017 Consensus of Evidence Statement drawn from the research in the field by the National Commission on Social, Emotional, and Academic Development (The Aspen Institute), authors Jones and Kahn state, "Children with stronger social and emotional competencies are also more likely to enter and graduate from college, succeed in their careers, have positive work and family relationships, better mental and physical health, reduced criminal behavior, and to become engaged citizens." Additionally, implementing social and emotional learning within a classroom setting can provide an inclusive climate and culture where learners of all walks of life can thrive—particularly neurodiverse learners; those who have experienced trauma, injustice, and/or discrimination; or have specific needs in terms of social, emotional, and behavioral development.

> **MYTH:** Regulation looks like a "calm" body.
>
> **REALITY:** Regulation can take many forms and takes into account our situation, task/job, and goals. Regulation might look like someone pumping themselves up for a big event, such as Michael Phelps swinging his arms and hitting his shoulder before a race. Regulation is controlling our impulse to act upon a triggering event and taking a second to think through our options before reacting. There is no one way that regulation looks!

While the landscape of social emotional learning includes numerous skills and competencies, I believe regulation is at the heart of all of them. Regulation is a foundational skill that we all need to successfully navigate life's trials and tribulations. Regulation provides us with a sense of wellness and achievement and sets us up to engage in healthy social interactions, work in collaboration with others, and contribute within our community. The Collaborative for Academic, Social, and Emotional Learning, commonly known as CASEL (www.casel.org), has established the widely adopted five core competencies of SEL for all educators:

CHAPTER 1: Regulation from the Inside Out

Zones Connection: CASEL

All of the CASEL five core competencies are addressed throughout *The Zones Digital Curriculum*, with the strongest emphasis on building self-awareness, self-management, and responsible decision-making. The Zones provides a framework and metacognitive pathway to help learners more independently understand, communicate, and manage their feelings with others, regulate to the demands of their environment(s), find adaptive ways to problem solve stressors, and meet their goals. Please refer to Appendix, page 130: *Zones of Regulation Digital Curriculum and CASEL Competency Correlation Chart* to find a correlation between SEL Core Competencies and The Zones Digital Curriculum to help inform and guide your instruction.

1. **Self-awareness:** Understanding self, including one's emotions, thoughts, values, strengths, and areas for potential growth. In addition, self-awareness allows one to understand the impact of their behavior within a particular context.

2. **Self-management:** The ability to regulate one's emotions, thoughts, and behavior while considering both personal and collective goals.

3. **Social awareness:** Involves taking perspective, showing compassion, and demonstrating empathy for others, including those with different cultures and backgrounds.

4. **Relationship skills:** Creating and maintaining healthy relations with others to negotiate social settings, including effective communication, working cohesively with a team, and conflict resolution.

5. **Responsible decision-making:** Weighing benefits vs. consequences of one's actions to make kind, healthy, responsible, and safe choices across a variety of situations.

BEYOND BEHAVIOR: UNDERSTANDING THE UNDERLYING FACTORS IMPACTING REGULATION

When I listen to *Car Talk* on NPR, I'm always amazed at the questions the hosts ask as they diagnose a car problem. They don't just consider what's under the hood, asking, *What does it sound like?* but they also probe about the driving terrain: *Where do you live? How many miles do you drive a week? What are the weather conditions? How long have you been driving? Who else drives the car?*

I've found that a similar approach to asking probing questions has helped me reframe how we should think about behavior. Looking under the hood of our learners can demystify some of their puzzling, dysregulated behaviors as well as inform the development of focused interventions, and can lead us to take actions that foster an environment where learners can thrive. I've witnessed many adults having a lightbulb moment when I talk to them about the sensory needs of a learner, allowing them a unique perspective on how the learner's sensory needs drive their behavior. When those needs aren't considered, many learners find less adaptive ways to get their sensory needs met that can appear as disruptive behavior to an untrained eye. In this section, I'm going to touch upon how the learner's core neurobiological components and lived experiences play a role in regulation.

FACTORS IMPACTING REGULATIONS

Later, I will discuss not only how we can take into account the learner's terrain, but also use strategies to smooth that terrain going forward.

WHAT'S UNDER THE HOOD: NEUROBIOLOGICAL CONSIDERATIONS IMPACTING REGULATION

When we look under a learner's hood, we need to first consider the role of the brain, body, and nervous system in relationship to regulation. Our nervous system serves as the command center for the body and is made up of the brain, spinal cord, and nerves throughout the body, relaying information to the brain about what is happening inside (and outside) the body, as well as sending out necessary commands in response to what it receives. I especially like how Daniel J. Siegel and Tina Payne Bryson, authors of *The Whole-Brain Child* (2011), broke down the brain's involvement in regulation in a very relatable way, referring to the "downstairs brain" that sits above the spinal cord and consists of the brain stem and limbic region (which includes the amygdala), and the "upstairs brain," which involves the prefrontal cortex. In the downstairs brain, we process and recognize powerful feelings, sensory input, instincts, and bodily functions. However, the downstairs brain doesn't provide guidance on how to handle what we're perceiving or sensing, including threats and fears. The downstairs brain's function is survival at all costs.

CHAPTER 1: Regulation from the Inside Out

The more evolved upstairs brain layers on the cognitive elements and executive functioning, such as thinking, imagining, planning, and perspective taking (the metacognitive strategies for regulation). Siegel and Bryson point out that, although the downstairs brain is well developed at birth, the upstairs brain doesn't fully develop until a person's mid-twenties. Therefore, they stress how important it is to have realistic expectations around regulation for our developing learners. For example, consider the following situation: Jorge, a 4-year-old, gets his truck taken away by a peer, and therefore hits him. Viewing this through Siegel and Bryson's lens, we can see that having his truck taken away activates his downstairs brain and shuts down his upstairs brain, or as Siegel and Bryson say, "isn't able to talk to his upstairs brain," so his attempt at regulation is hitting his peer. In the moment when his downstairs brain is firing, he simply doesn't have access to his developing upstairs brain where the thinking, problem solving, and planning occur. Taking a closer look at the developmental nature of regulation strategies can help us make more sense of why Jorge hit his peer rather than ask for his truck back or just walk away.

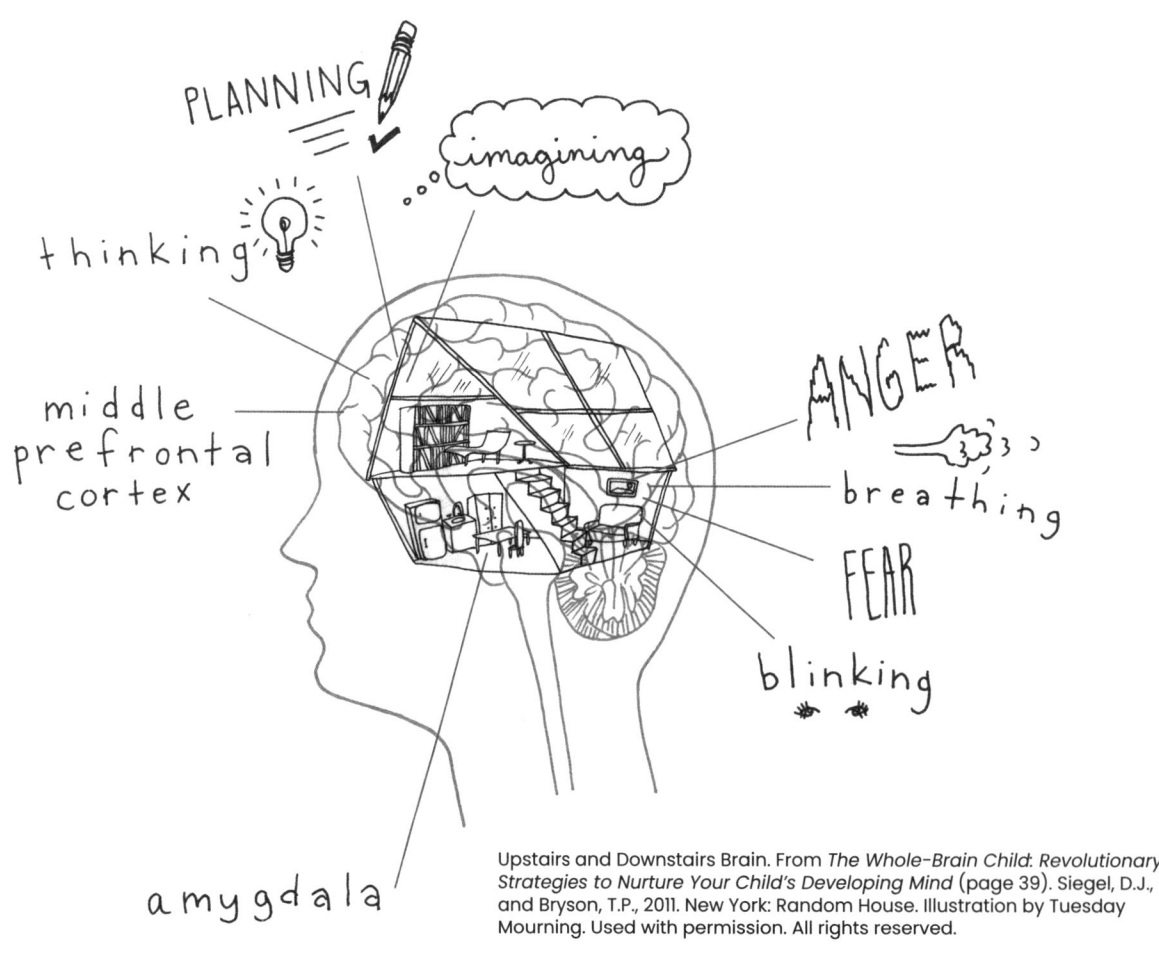

Upstairs and Downstairs Brain. From *The Whole-Brain Child: Revolutionary Strategies to Nurture Your Child's Developing Mind* (page 39). Siegel, D.J., and Bryson, T.P., 2011. New York: Random House. Illustration by Tuesday Mourning. Used with permission. All rights reserved.

Developmental Nature of Regulation Strategies

Regulation is developmental, like learning to walk and talk. Some learners are neurobiologically wired to develop regulation competencies at a different rate than others. Regulation development does not necessarily correlate with a learner's age, intellect, or verbal abilities. To help us understand how learners are progressing in their regulation development continuum, I find the three stages of regulation strategies laid out in *The SCERTS© Model* (Prizant et al., 2006) particularly useful:

STAGE 1: Behavior Strategies

Simple motor actions or sensory-motor inputs to cope, soothe, or regulate alertness.

WHEN: Predominate in the first year of life in neurotypical development.

EXAMPLES: A baby fusses and uses oral-motor thumb sucking to self-sooth, wails when needing to be fed, or swats away/hits at something irritating them. The infant is heavily dependent on co-regulators being attuned to their needs and helping them with these strategies, such as a caregiver providing the sensory motor input to support regulation by rocking, massaging, swaddling, singing, or bringing them to their food source to be fed.

STAGE 2: Language Strategies

Using language (spoken word/approximations, gestures, signs, symbols, non-verbal communication, assistive communication devices) to support regulation and organize behavior. Language strategies include being able to share how one is feeling, such as communicating with a caregiver when they feel angry or sad.

WHEN: May emerge during late infancy/toddler years; express basic feelings around 3 years of age in neurotypical development.

EXAMPLES: When irritated by a peer, the child says "stop" or shakes head "no" when presented with something they don't like; when hungry, asks, points, or gestures for bottle rather than wails.

STAGE 3: Metacognitive Strategies

Using higher-level thinking; integrating in self-talk and knowledge of self, their experiences, and the world to problem solve, plan, reflect, and reason to support regulation of feelings and behavior.

WHEN: May emerge around the age of 3–4 in neurotypical development and continues to develop and become more refined through one's life span.

EXAMPLES: A girl feels hurt when she learns she was excluded from a sleepover, but then can reason that her friend is only allowed to have one friend sleep over at a time, so she might have a turn another time; consciously taking a deep breath when tagged out in a game and following the rules so they can return to play again quickly.

CHAPTER 1: Regulation from the Inside Out

Zones Connection: Regulation Development

The concepts taught in *The Zones of Regulation® Digital Curriculum* help learners use more sophisticated language and metacognitive regulation strategies by providing an easy communication and visual system to express how they are feeling, as well as a metacognitive framework to help them regulate.

We shouldn't presume that all learners in the same classroom, or grade, are in the same place; regulation skills need to be assessed and not assumed. For example, some learners can have conversations with you about many things and openly share their personal experiences; however, some learners, such as Jorge from the earlier example, in their stage of regulation strategies development have limited insights into their feelings and limited strategies to manage them. Jorge often uses behavior strategies to regulate his distress, such as hitting others, running out of the room, or hiding from staff. Although very communicative, he is only beginning to develop language strategies to communicate his feelings, and he has even less access to the higher-level metacognitive skills that would help him problem solve and regulate with more ease.

There is no clear progression from one stage of strategies to the next, and development is impacted by one's cognition, linguistic growth, and guidance from caregivers. Although the stages of regulation strategies build in sophistication and emerge over time, we adults still use behavior and language strategies to regulate when it serves us well, like chewing on a pen cap in a meeting to remain focused (a behavior strategy). And there will be times where we (YES, even us adults) have our upstairs brains hijacked by the big feelings in our downstairs brain, interfering with our ability to use metacognitive strategies, and inadvertently use less-sophisticated strategies to cope with a stressor. For example, when facing a conflict, adults may use angry words (a language strategy) or slam the door (a behavior strategy), rather than using thought-out, reflective, metacognitive strategies. As we move on to learn about underlying factors affecting regulation, continue to consider where the learner is in the development of their regulation strategies.

There are underlying critical neurobiological components that assist in the orchestration of regulation in the brain and body. The following neurobiological components can impact how the upstairs brain and downstairs brain learn how to communicate with each other, as well as play a role in developing more sophisticated regulation strategies.

1. Sensory processing (including interoception)
2. Executive functioning
3. Emotional regulation
4. Social cognition

Each of these processes is briefly described and illustrated in the figure (opposite): Neurobiological Components of Regulation. In addition, I also discuss the role of reading context and cognitive prediction, as well as how trauma exposure impacts the nervous system.

Getting Into The **Zones** of Regulation

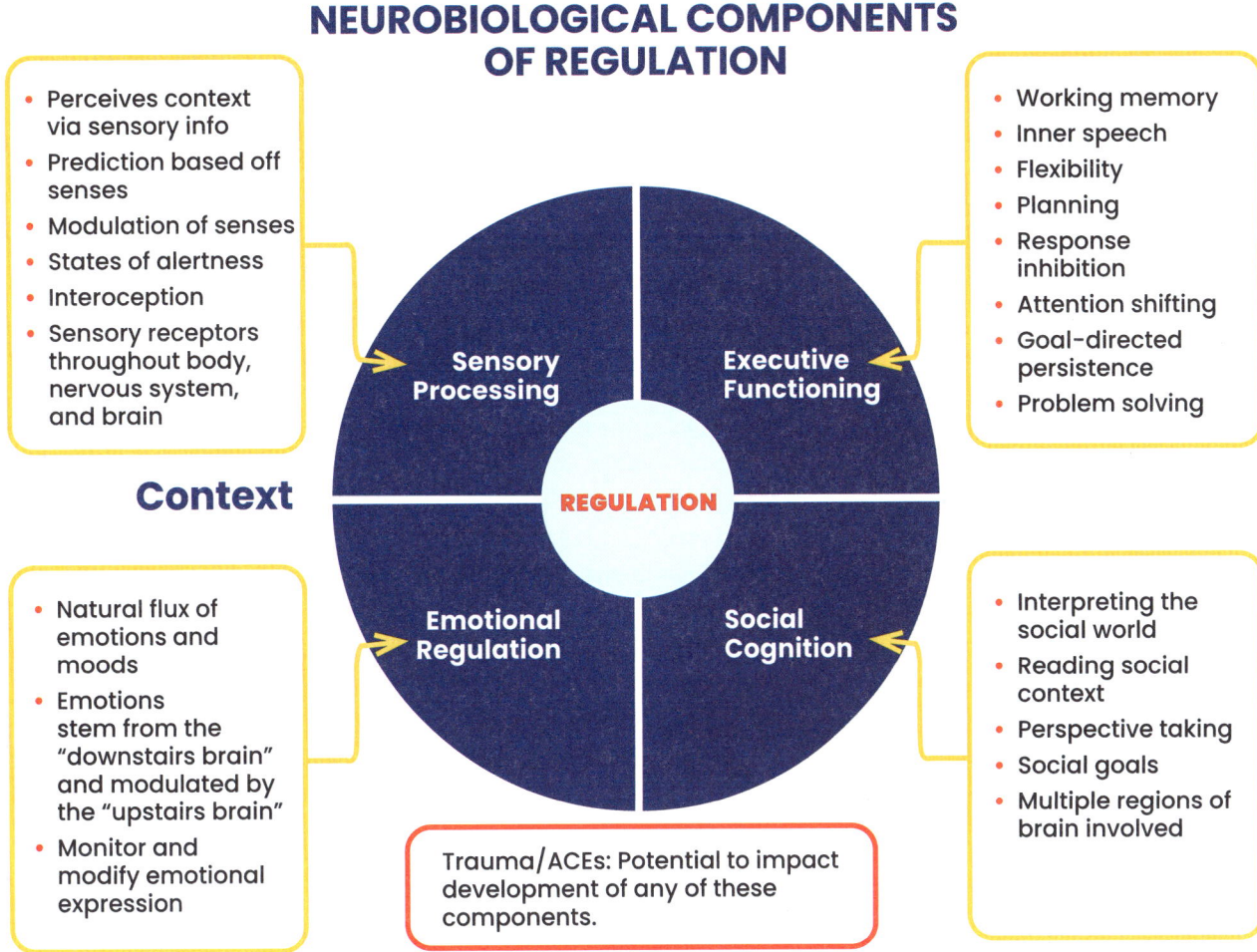

Sensory Processing and Interoception

The first component, sensory processing, describes how sensory information is perceived by your senses and relayed via your nervous system to your downstairs brain, as well as how you make sense of the information in your upstairs brain. Sensory processing is something we all do, yet how we process and integrate our senses is unique to each of us.

THE ROLE OF SENSORY PROCESSING We integrate sensory information from the five senses (taste, touch, smell, vision, hearing) as well as the lesser talked about senses—vestibular (balance), proprioceptive (body location and position), and interoception (body sensations)—to make predictions and meet a purpose. For example, as we hear someone's voice near us, the brain registers the sensory input of the sound along with visual stimuli, and predicts someone is talking to us. At other times we want to ignore sensory information to prevent becoming overwhelmed or distracted, such as blocking out noise from outside as we try to fall asleep.

CHAPTER 1: Regulation from the Inside Out

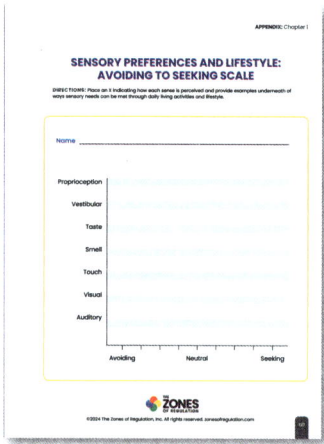

Additional Resources

For learners who need deeper support in building awareness and understanding of interoceptive body signals:

- *The Interoception Curriculum: A Step-by-Step Guide to Developing Mindful Self-Regulation* (K. Mahler, 2019) is an excellent resource and can be used in conjunction with The Zones of Regulation.
- *The Alert Program* (Williams and Shellenberger, 1996) is a well-regarded and valuable teaching resource that provides in-depth exploration on how we process our senses and provides sensory-based supports for regulation.
- For further information about sensory processing, *Sensational Kids: Hope and Help for Children with Sensory Processing Disorder* (Miller, 2014)
- *The Out-of-Sync Child: Recognizing and Coping with Sensory Processing Differences,* 3rd ed. (Kranowitz, 2022).

PROCESSING SENSORY STIMULI We all have different thresholds for how our senses process stimuli and what feels like the just-right amount of sensory information for the brain and body to feel organized and regulated. Sometimes there is a high threshold for one or more of the senses, causing us to crave and seek intense input from that sense to feel regulated. For example, I think of Aahana who was always on the go and could only sit for short periods of time before feeling restless. Finding a purposeful and meaningful way for Aahana to meet her sensory needs was important for her body's internal state to feel regulated. Aahana needed additional movement—which she got through classroom jobs, a wobble stool, and high-impact activity such as jumping onto a crash pad prior to a focus activity—for her to be in an optimal state for learning. On the other hand, sometimes a threshold is set low for one or more of the senses, causing avoidance to sensory input. I remember Tony, who could only tolerate minimal auditory input before he became overwhelmed and his body felt uncomfortable. Giving Tony a way to control the sound, such as providing noise-reduction headphones and easy access to a space in the classroom away from all the commotion, helped him regulate. The Sensory Preferences and Lifestyle tracker (Appendix, page 127) can be used as a self-reflection or learner-reflection exercise to consider where one falls on the continuum, from avoiding to seeking, with the various senses and lifestyle choices made to accommodate sensory preferences.

FILTERING SENSORY INPUT Sensory processing also includes filtering the sensory input you receive so that you aren't bombarded by all the irrelevant stimuli in your environment (often referred to as modulation). For example, a learner in the classroom has the relevant stimuli they need to process (such as the teacher giving instructions and work in front of them) but may be overwhelmed by all the background sensory input they have difficulty filtering out (such as itchy tags on their clothing, noise from the hallway, excessive artwork/visuals hung in the classroom, smell coming from the lunchroom). Filtering sensory information can be effortless for some but exhausting for others, taxing their body's nervous system and regulation capacity. They may appear distracted, irritated, restless, fatigued, or shut down/withdrawn.

What Is Interoception? One of the senses, interoception, is so closely tied to regulation that it deserves a conversation of its own. Kelly Mahler, an expert in the field, defines it as "the sense that allows us to answer the question, *'How do I feel?'* in any given moment." She explains that the ability to detect and understand body signals such as a racing heart, tense muscles, or a growling stomach is an important foundation of regulation (*Interoception*, 2015).

Getting Into The **Zones** of Regulation

From *The Road to Regulation,* by Leah Kuypers and Elizabeth Sautter, (Think Social Publishing, 2021)

INTEROCEPTION is the collection of senses providing information about the internal state of the body.

EXECUTIVE FUNCTIONING (EF) is a general term that describes the cognitive processes involved in the conscious control of thoughts and actions that help us accomplish our goals.

Neuroscientists have found that interoception is an integral component of the emotional experience, as our body signals provide important clues to exactly how we are feeling or what emotion we are experiencing in any given moment. (See storybook image above.) Therefore, it's essential to teach learners to notice their own personal body signals so that they have reliable clues to inform how they are feeling and what they need to comfort their body. The interoceptive system informs us when the balance of our body's internal state is off, taxing our regulation capacity. Think about having an exhausting day at work, and then consider how much capacity you would have to regulate the emotional stressors at home. Noticing our body signals can alert us to take actions that help us regulate (such as taking a warm bath or drinking a cup of tea to unwind) and re-establish our

Zones Connection: Sensory Processing and Interoception

The Zones Digital Curriculum addresses interoception and building self-awareness of sensory information in Concepts 4 and 5 by exploring the body signals associated with each of The Zones, understanding what the learner's body is communicating about their feelings and internal states, while building the language/communication associated to label and identify feelings. The Zones of Regulation integrates meaningful sensory-based supports that we call "regulation tools." Learners explore when and how to access these sensory-based tools from their " Zones Toolbox" to help maintain and adjust their internal states and energy—that is, their Zones.

13

CHAPTER 1: Regulation from the Inside Out

Zones Connection: Executive Functioning

Various executive functions, such as inner speech, flexible thinking, planning, problem solving, and inhibition, are addressed in *The Zones of Regulation® Digital Curriculum*. Learners develop self-awareness, purposeful decision-making, and a skill set of executive functioning strategies that support healthy regulation. These strategies cultivate learners' ability to more consciously mediate their thoughts and actions. In turn, this metacognitive awareness leads to increased control and problem-solving abilities. The Zones of Regulation Pathway outlined in the next chapter highlights the metacognitive thinking we construct to help us figure out how best to regulate in a context and reflect on the effect.

balance and coping capacity. In other words, knowing when we need to regulate our bodies and doing so helps us manage our emotions and behaviors.

For some learners, sensory processing and interoception differences may be an under-the-hood factor to consider that impacts their regulation abilities. For example, Samuel sought proprioceptive sensory input to feel comfortable and regulated. However, his teacher held him to the same standards as her other kindergarten learners and didn't accommodate for his differences. Samuel found ways to support his sensory needs and regulated them by bumping into other kids as he lined up and rocking in his chair. This felt good to him but was seen as aggressive or disruptive behavior by his teacher. By considering what was under the hood for Samuel, his teacher was able to reframe how she interpreted Samuel's behavior and collaborated with him and his team to help him access sensory tools to support his regulation. As you can see, considering sensory processing needs can help shift one's lens from seeing behavior, to understanding how to support regulation for some learners.

Executive Functioning

Sometimes referred to as cognitive control, executive functioning (EF) is a general term that describes the cognitive processes involved in the conscious control of thoughts and actions that help us accomplish our goals. In other words, it's the thinking behind the doing that takes place in the pre-frontal cortex located in the "upstairs brain." Executive functioning is like a command or control center in our brains that oversees our behavior and mental operations. Numerous mental operations fall under EF. Some that are influential in developing more metacognitive self-regulatory capacity are:

- **Working memory:** Accessing, updating, and purging "information files" in the brain. This helps us use past experiences to guide our thinking, actions, and reactions.
- **Inner speech:** Using self-talk, interpersonal dialogues, and reflection
- **Flexibility:** Considering multiple options and applying different rules in different settings
- **Planning:** Organizing actions and executing a plan to reach desired goals
- **Response inhibition:** Setting priorities, motivation, and resisting impulses
- **Attention shifting:** Attending to two or more activities simultaneously, such as taking notes while listening to a lecture

- **Goal-directed persistence:** Working toward a goal despite hurdles and distractions
- **Problem solving:** Brainstorming solutions and identifying the best option

Peg Dawson and Richard Guare, experts in executive functioning and authors of *Executive Skills in Children and Adolescents*, 3rd ed. (2018), point out these skills, which are at the heart of self-regulation and self-control, unfold over time and continue to develop well into adolescence and early adulthood. As these executive functions develop, learners become better equipped for the metacognitive thinking and problem solving necessary to overcome the challenges they meet and to regulate the emotions they experience. For example, I think of Xavier, age 9, who often responded to school stressors, such as challenging work or a redirection by a teacher, with an impulsive swiping of the contents off the table or desk. His self-talk was defeating: "I'm so stupid." Over the course of the school year, Xavier learned that his self-talk wasn't helping and began to replace it with a more nurturing voice (inner speech), "This is hard, I can take a break." He developed more metacognitive strategies that helped him catch and override his impulse to swipe the table clear when frustrated (response inhibition). Through exploration and with practice, he became more skilled in accessing and using his regulation tools (requiring problem solving, planning, and goal-directed persistence) to manage his feelings. As Xavier's example illustrates, there is a strong relationship between executive functioning and regulation. It is important to note that development of EF skills can be impacted by relationships, adverse environments, and trauma (Harvard's Center on the Developing Child, 2021 https://developingchild.harvard.edu/science/key-concepts/executive-function/). I discuss this in more detail later.

Emotional Regulation

Aristotle put it wisely: "Anyone can become angry, that is easy...but to be angry with the right person, to the right degree, at the right time, for the right purpose, and in the right way...this is not easy." Emotional regulation includes all the processes that are responsible for managing our emotional reactions to meet a goal, such as the one Aristotle illustrates in this example. This management gives us the ability to become aware of, monitor, and have a sense of control over our emotions. Emotional regulation is part of "emotional literacy," which involves understanding and regulating one's own feelings. It's also being able to notice, listen, and empathize with others' feelings, resolve emotional problems, and relate emotionally with others.

FEELINGS: The signals, emotions, and energy within our body.

EMOTIONS: How we label and talk about our feelings.

CHAPTER 1: Regulation from the Inside Out

Zones Connection: Emotional Regulation

The Zones of Regulation is a valuable tool for making sense of, organizing, and labeling what the downstairs brain springs upon us and integrating the upstairs brain to help us metacognitively manage this information. In essence, as leaders, we are strengthening communication (or building the staircase as Siegel and Bryson put it) between the upstairs and downstairs brain.

The Zones of Regulation® Digital Curriculum incorporates principles of Cognitive and Dialectic Behavior Therapy (CBT/DBT)—common, metacognitively based, therapeutic methodologies to aid in emotional regulation. These approaches address increasing emotional and behavioral awareness, as well as monitoring, modifying, and evaluating one's emotional response, including the timing, duration, and intensity of our feelings so we can do something difficult with more ease.

Managing emotions and feelings doesn't mean eliminating them. In fact, we always feel something. Feelings are innate and are part of the human experience. Sometimes people categorize feelings as either "positive" or "negative." I prefer to categorize them as "comfortable" or "uncomfortable," acknowledging that feeling sad or angry doesn't feel good, while eliminating the judgmental tone of "negative." Russell Barkley, an internationally recognized authority on ADHD, describes in his research that emotions are automatically triggered in response to events, and this happens in our "downstairs brain." For example, I hear a loud bang and my downstairs brain fires out fear. However, metacognitive elements from the "upstairs brain," such as those described in the executive functioning section, as well as incorporating objectivity, motivation, and understanding others' perspectives, help provide more sophistication in how we regulate the emotion. Rather than running to hide, I reason, "That noise was probably the loose porch door swinging in the wind. I'm safe." And I go on to take a couple of deep breaths to relax. The fear is still there, but I've managed it.

Rather than telling someone how they should or should not feel, ("don't be mad/sad" or "don't worry") we, as leaders, need to accept all the feelings that our learners experience and create safe and healthy ways for them to experience and express these feelings. An all-too-common response to emotions is learners avoiding (and even "masking") them, which leads to unhealthy behaviors and poor emotional wellness. When we support learners in experiencing their full range of emotions, while creating safety for them, we can help them better manage the discomfort that comes with these emotions. This important step can lead to learning how to express your emotions.

Let's consider this example: Misha worried about many things, and sometimes she expressed her worry as anger. When it was time for swim lessons, she stomped around shouting, "I hate swimming." At first, I was surprised by Misha's reaction because she previously showed that she loved swim lessons. Instead of reminding her, "You always love swimming," which requires use of her upstairs brain that she doesn't currently have access to, I responded by calming my nervous system first. I told her I was going to take a deep breath. Then, I sat beside Misha and validated her feelings with my actions. I used a non-threatening stance, and gently said, "Sounds like you're upset about having to go to swim lessons." Together, we regulated the big feelings as she took some more deep breaths with me. When I circled back around with Misha, she expressed she was scared to go to swim lessons because she had recently gotten her ears pierced and feared she would lose an earring swimming, causing her pierced hole to close. Rather than telling her, "Don't worry," we talked about what would happen if her earring fell out and, in the worst case, her piercing closed. Misha acknowledged that it didn't hurt all that much to get her ear pierced and she could do it again if she had to. She also hated missing swim lessons, which she enjoyed. This emotional co-regulation around her anxiety helped Misha get back to her love of swimming. By supporting Misha in being able to safely experience her full range of emotions, I helped her manage her emotions.

Without applying this educational neuroscience lens, we may miss out on opportunities to support learners through their challenges. If I wasn't able to help Misha regulate and express her worries, and I only looked at her surface behavior, I would have been focused on her anger and her stomping. I may have taken a disciplinarian approach and even suggested a consequence if she didn't go swimming. This would have reinforced avoiding the anxiety. And when we respond to anxiety with avoidance, it increases their anxiety, making it even harder to do the challenging thing they were worried about. Reacting without looking under the hood could have led me to contributing to the creation of a huge barrier about swimming for Misha. Instead, she strengthened her regulation and problem-solving pathways in her brain and got right back to the pool!

Social Cognition

Social cognition refers to how we take in, make sense of, remember, and apply information about the social world around us, including interpreting the social behavior of ourselves and others in a situation. We use our social cognition when connecting with our family and friends, but it is also at play when we encounter strangers within community spaces. Social cognition is a neurobiological component that begins developing at birth and is integral to regulating when we are in community with others, which is where we spend much of our lives.

As we gain greater awareness of the social world, our socially driven motivation helps us connect with others and meet societal norms while also maintaining a sense of our own individuality. Social cognition is at play when we:

1. Think about or perceive others in a situation: *Someone is walking toward a building door with their arms full. Their intent must be to carry their load inside.*

2. Relate it to what we have come to know about people in the world: *It's hard to open a door while carrying a big load.*

> Rather than telling someone how they should or should not feel, ("don't be mad/sad" or "don't worry") we, as leaders, need to accept all the feelings that our learners experience and create safe and healthy ways for them to experience and express these feelings.

CHAPTER 1: Regulation from the Inside Out

3. Consider others' perspectives: *It would be helpful and kind to open the door for them. It is likely they would feel grateful.*

4. Use all this information to guide our own actions and reactions: *Move ahead of them to open the door for them.*

> **SOCIAL THINKING AND REGULATION**
>
> To help address social goals around building social cognitive competencies, the Social Thinking Methodology® (www.socialthinking.com) developed by Michelle Garcia Winner can help learners interpret social context, understand perspective, and build relationships. This work may be beneficial for those looking to deepen their understanding of how to regulate around social goals while exploring one's personal expectations in addition to societal norms.

It can be challenging for learners who have differences in quickly reading and interpreting social cues and context to navigate the social world, and these differences may contribute to dysregulation. For example, Tory is sitting at their desk drawing and sees their teacher look directly at them; however, they're not sure what the teacher's body language and facial expression are communicating. As a result, they become stressed and confused.

When determining how to regulate, social cognition factors into the equation as one becomes aware of and considers the people in the context, societal norms, and one's social goals. Say a learner enters the crowded lunchroom hoping to catch up with friends (social goal). However, his tray tips and food spills on him, causing him distress and embarrassment. Using his social cognition (in coordination with his executive functioning and emotional regulation) he reminds himself he can still sit with his friends once cleaned up and overrides the urge to run out of the cafeteria. He uses a self-regulation tool (i.e., deep breathing or self-talk) to help him work toward his social goal of catching up with his friends. A moment later, a friend comes over to help him pick up his food, co-regulating

Zones Connection: Social Cognition

The Zones Digital Curriculum weaves social cognitive elements in to foster understanding of this social emotional process and increase independence in regulation. Instruction begins by exploring multiple perspectives learners might have to the same situation and comparing and contrasting our body signals, feelings, and Zones with others to reinforce that we each have a unique brain and body. This sets the stage for learners (and leaders) to be aware of all the different ways regulation can look and feel, rather than teaching to a socially prescribed standard—such as only when we have a "calm" looking body that sits "square in a chair" are we considered "on task" or a "good listener." These concepts are essential to building a climate that supports regulation and well-being over compliance. The Zones also addresses how each learner has regulation tools unique to them and provides agency for the learner in identifying and using them.

with him. All of these elements (context, societal norms, and social goals) came into play for this learner.

For The Zones of Regulation to be successful, you need to honor your learner's authentic self, or who they truly are as a person, and create a safe space for them that values both their strengths and differences. Rather than teaching to preconceived notions of societal norms, which can cause harm and stress for neurodivergent and linguistically and culturally diverse learners, we need to understand learners' goals for themselves in relation to the social world and have this understanding drive instruction. Consider Marco who has a repetitive stim routine that involves him circling around while flapping his hands. The flapping is a calming strategy that allows him to be in a more regulated state. Rather than trying to keep Marco from doing the stim and causing him undue stress, we can embrace it as a powerful regulation tool and use examples like this to educate staff and peers on diverse ways learners can regulate. Welcoming Marco's regulation strategies sets up an environment where he can be himself, use his strengths, and regulate while also meeting the demands of his school day.

Context and Prediction

The four neurobiological processes discussed earlier operate in our brains while we also take into account the context or situation. This includes who is around, what is happening, and when and where it is taking place. Situations are fluid, meaning they are constantly unfolding and affecting what our senses take in, the emotions they evoke, and the executive functions and social cognition used to navigate them. For example, you're on the school bus approaching the school, and you see (sensory processing) a lengthy line of buses ahead of yours waiting to pull into the drop off zone. This stirs up worries (emotional regulation) of being late for class. However, you realize there are lots of other kids in all the other buses waiting too (social cognition). You use your self-talk to remind yourself, "I won't be the only person late," and plan ways to save time at your locker (executive functions). As humans, we constantly predict what will likely happen within a context based on what we know and have experienced in the past. The mind integrates the information from the senses and uses these predictive models to make a logical guess about what will likely happen in our context, helping us feel more at ease and prepared for what is to come (J. Hohwy, *The Predictive Mind*, 2013).

When we predict a context incorrectly, such as expecting to be on time to school but discovering you will have to wait to get to the

Zones Connection: Context and Prediction

The Zones of Regulation® Digital Curriculum teaches learners to become more aware of reading and interpreting context in the situations unfolding around them, as well as identifying their triggers and sparks (prediction errors) that can lead to dysregulation. In addition, learners strategize and plan for how to cope with unanticipated changes and triggers.

CHAPTER 1: Regulation from the Inside Out

> ### What Are ACEs?
>
> Adverse childhood experiences, or ACEs, are potentially traumatic events that occur in childhood (0–17 years). For example:
>
> - Experiencing violence, abuse, or neglect
> - Witnessing violence in the home or community
> - Having a family member attempt or die by suicide
>
> ACEs also include aspects of the child's environment that can undermine their sense of safety, stability, and bonding, like growing up in a household with:
>
> - Substance use problems
> - Mental health problems
> - Instability due to parental separation or household members being in jail or prison
>
> Please note the examples above are not meant to be a complete list of adverse experiences. There are many other traumatic experiences that could impact health and well-being.
>
> From Adverse Childhood Experiences (ACEs) (cdc.gov)

drop off zone, our brain registers this as a "prediction error" that can trigger uncomfortable feelings, such as stress or anxiety and a heightened state of alertness. Another example of a prediction error would be expecting to see your teacher when you arrive at school but instead discovering there is a substitute.

When we are less familiar or uncertain in a context, we become more vigilant with our senses, taking in an abundance of information, which can also lead us to feel overwhelmed and in a heightened state of alertness. This can also lead to misinterpreting neutral or positive information as threatening, which can also increase our state of alertness. An example of this is getting dropped off on the first day at a new, unfamiliar school and getting overwhelmed or flustered trying to find your locker or a classroom. As you can see through these examples, context and prediction can be complicated, but it's essential to consider as you work to understand your learner and make sense of what is "under the hood."

Trauma and the Nervous System

Trauma and adverse childhood experiences (ACEs) can potentially impact one's regulatory system and disrupt social, emotional, and cognitive skill development. According to the Centers for Disease Control and Prevention (CDC), children's brain development can be impacted by the toxic stress induced by ACEs which, in turn, can affect abilities in attention, decision-making, learning, and response to stress (2021).

Stephen Porges' work on polyvagal theory (2011) helps us understand how our body and brain work together via the nervous system to respond to different situations, particularly ones that include stress, trauma, and/or danger. Porges has specifically identified the vagus nerve's involvement in regulation, social connection, and fear response. The vagus nerve is a cranial nerve that is responsible for coordinating bodily responses to protect us from danger and keep us safe (such as heart rate, breathing, digestion, and emotional states) even before we consciously think about it. This "mobilization" is all part of our Autonomic Nervous System (ANS); however, this nerve is prone to damage when one endures chronic stress, ACEs, and/or trauma and results in people quickly and inadvertently moving to heightened physiological states of alertness (often referred to as "fight or flight") when they perceive threats in their environment. When we sense we can't defend ourselves by the initial sympathetic state of "fight or flight" in a situation, we then move into a dorsal vagal state of "freeze," "shutdown," or appeasement. This secondary "collapse" response state results from feeling overwhelmed by the threat and can happen quite quickly or over a period of time. These reflexive, autonomic responses form what Porges refers to as the "safety-threat detection system" that serves as protective behavior to the individual and happens subconsciously. Porges calls the third response state the "social engagement" response, where the ventral vagus nerve is activated and we feel safe, connected, and relaxed.

Appeasement is protective behavior, in response to trauma, that describes the attempt to avoid conflict or trauma by aiming to please others. Take Sienna, for example. She often presents herself as well regulated, overachieving, and compliant. But internally she always works to manage the constant threat of others' disapproval. Appeasement, such as Sienna's, can stem from mistreatment by an adult. Appeasement can be exhausting for the learner, taking a toll on their regulation capacity as they ignore their own needs (such as asking to use the bathroom) and place others before themselves (because they don't want to inconvenience the teacher). Once in a safe space, such as at home, learners like Sienna often emotionally and behaviorally fall apart.

As adults, we can reframe how we see a learner's behavior, understanding that the behavior is not intentional or by choice, but rather results from a stressor or trigger that elicits their instinct to survive. The behavior strategies they use to regulate (such as bolting out of the classroom, becoming aggressive, flopping to the ground) happen at the ANS (Autonomic Nervous System) level through their inherent threat detection system. Our job as leaders is to support the learner by providing cues of safety through co-regulation to help the learner's ANS receive messages that the present moment is actually safe. Once we understand the cause of the response, we can explore ways to support the learner, smoothing the terrain by removing triggers, modifying a task, or adapting a material or environment. In addition, we can collaboratively develop a plan that fosters the learner's skills and capabilities with the support of a safe, co-regulating adult.

One learner I worked with would seemingly go from a calm, relaxed state to being aggressive, but only with a certain staff member. This staff member smelled of cigarette smoke. The learner's abusive father was also a smoker. We theorized this learner was perceiving this staff member as a threat due to the smell association and this subconsciously triggered a protective fight state. Once we were able to understand this, we used our interventions and co-regulatory strategies to help promote a sense of safety for the learner. At the same time, we modified their schedule so they were paired with another staff member.

In a similar way, when we heard from Sienna's parents about the dysregulation that was happening at home, we problem-solved with them and Sienna to discover how hard she was working to regulate at school and identified ways to support her so her regulation was easier. We built time into her day to check in with trusted adults, and examined classroom management systems to determine if they were exacerbating the stress for her. In both examples, understanding how trauma impacts what's going on under the hood helped us make sense of these learners' regulation challenges. In the next chapter we will discuss how The Zones of Regulation helps leaders understand what state the learners are in and explore the intersection between Zones and the polyvagal theory.

As we look under the hood, it is commonly recognized that learners born with neurobiological or developmental differences, such as autism and ADHD, have a higher association with regulation differences. We also must consider the impact of trauma and ACEs on one's regulatory system and social, emotional, and cognitive skill development. Everyone who has divergent regulation abilities does not have a diagnosis or disability, and it is important to remember that regulation is developmental in nature. It is long overdue that the conversation is shifting to how to support learners with regulation differences vs. labeling them with unhelpful terms such as attention-seeking, manipulative, lazy, or naughty. Considering "what is under the hood" provides us with direction on how to focus interventions aimed at fostering regulation abilities.

WHAT'S THE TERRAIN: THE IMPACT OF LIVED EXPERIENCE ON REGULATION

All of us have a unique story composed of our lived experiences. Earlier we referred to this in our car analogy as the "terrain": the impacting external factors such as weather, road conditions, traffic, and directions. Each learner also experiences an external terrain that potentially impacts their regulation. If we view learners through a narrow lens, focusing on their behavior or their disabilities, we only see a small piece of their story. We can miss not only the "why" behind a learner's social and emotional development but also their strengths and assets.

We use a broader lens to define the terrain, which includes the impact of culture and systems that can significantly shape our learner's lives, growth, and development. When diving into this work, it is crucial that we view our learner's experiences through a critical equity lens. Deeply ingrained biases such as racism, ableism, sexism, homophobia, and transphobia have serious effects and consequences for our learners across educational and community settings.

Each learner's terrain can include features that could help them navigate it with more ease. These features might be:

- A supportive, tight-knit community
- A caregiver who fiercely advocates
- A belief system that bestows values
- A family narrative that features stories of resilience

All of these features can positively impact our learners and shape their identity.

Some of our learners have encountered challenging terrain that includes many bumps (and even boulders) in the road, which shaped them in becoming the person they are today. Some lived experiences, such as poverty, a traumatic event, and chronic stress or illness, can take a toll on our learners and impact their ability to regulate. We need to keep ACEs (as referenced earlier) in mind and recognize they are common across all populations. Almost two-thirds of the CDC's ACEs study participants reported at least one ACE, and more than one in five reported three or more ACEs. Remember that a compounding of ACEs can impact one's neurobiology and affect how a learner perceives and manages a stressor in the moment.

Rather than assume our good intentions will help all learners regardless of the terrain they've experienced, we can seek to understand their past and current experiences within settings in which they have spent time. These might include alternative school placements or detention centers, as well as a classroom, child-care program, or home. For example, a learner who has been kicked out of multiple schools may feel jaded and distrustful of staff in their educational setting, putting up a protective barrier that may come across as disinterested or defensive.

Understanding a learner's past can inform and guide our instruction and interventions, creating a smoother terrain going forward. Some factors to consider in more depth that contribute to one's terrain follow, however, this overview is not meant to be comprehensive.

Relationships

Mona Delahooke (2017) explains the development of regulation for a child is dependent on responsive caregivers who help to manage (co-regulate) the child's emotional states as an infant and toddler until the child can learn to self-regulate. Expanding on Porges' work in polyvagal theory, Delahooke says a loving and warm relationship can often help the developing child to be in a calm, alert "social engagement" response state where learning is possible, providing a foundation for future possibilities. Zaretta Hammond explains in *Culturally Responsive Teaching & the Brain* (2015) that relationships aren't just emotional, they also involve a physical component that impacts the brain and body. Positive relationships can help turn off the safety-threat detection system in the downstairs brain and stop the body from sending out the stress hormones that make learning and regulating more difficult. One powerful way we can learn about the terrain our learners have navigated is by establishing a relationship with our learners and their caregivers. For some, this can be a challenge and require more time to connect if their defense strategies are activated based on their experiences.

> Consider that many learners have caregivers who provide loving, healthy relationships, yet the learner's neurobiology is impacting regulation development. Avoid blaming or shaming caregivers for a learner's regulation challenges.

Culture

Hammond (2015) explains that culture is the way the brain, regardless of race, disability, or ethnicity, makes sense of the world, "turn[ing] everyday happenings into meaningful events" (p. 22). Culture explains many of the unspoken rules around social norms and social behavior, such as eye contact, personal space, and voice volume levels.

Culture also impacts what behaviors we perceive as hostile, offensive, or a threat. For example, in some cultures people stand close together to communicate; in other cultures someone coming close to you may be perceived as aggressive and invading your personal space rather than as a friendly initiation of communication. There may be vast differences between a set of norms, values, linguistics, and expected behaviors established in a setting such as a school than those of the learner's home. How a learner acts or responds may be a norm within their culture but not align with the majority culture of the setting.

Take for example a learner who comes from an autistic culture that uses less eye contact when directly communicating. A learner's actions or responses can lead to misinterpretations—and even unwarranted discipline measures—when there are cultural differences. This learner is misperceived as disrespectful or disengaged by a teacher who teaches in a culture where eye contact is expected.

This is often referred to as cultural dissonance and can serve as a stressor for the individual (Banks and Obiakor, 2015). When this is the case, the terrain is not culturally neutral, thus creating stressors and obstacles on the journey for learners with cultural and linguistic differences that pull from their regulation capacity. Here it's the confusion or upset feelings the learner experiences when his teacher sternly tells him to look him in the eyes when speaking to him.

Sociopolitical Environment

The world we live in is far from "fair." It is no secret that our society has vast and longstanding inequities that disproportionally impact people of certain races, gender identities, classes, languages, neurotypes, and abilities. People experiencing inequities have many disadvantages in their terrain, especially in critical areas such as housing, transportation, education, and health care.

More unfair is that some people, most of them white, get access to privileges in these areas they don't do anything to earn. They get easy approval for a housing loan, a job interview, access to better schools, or freedom to shop without scrutiny (Hammond, 2015). It's important that we educate ourselves as well as recognize and validate how these disparities and inequities (including segregation that leads to better housing and schools for some) have impacted our learners—the oppression they have experienced and the trauma these inequities may have caused. If we are more aware and conscious of these broader social injustices, we can better understand and support our learners (Ashley, D., 2015).

Once, referring to our car and terrain analogy, one of our collaborators said, "They didn't even design a car for my road." He went on to explain that the collective experience that many people of color like him faced during their education in schools didn't reflect and value their identity. He felt he was never able to express negative emotions for fear of being labeled an angry Black boy who was seen as a discipline problem.

This is equally true for neurodivergent learners who may have experienced complex terrains. They may be rejected or excluded by peers and adults, and are often left out of the conversation around equity and inclusion. Ultimately, these sociopolitical factors can result in harm, stress, and trauma as learners try to navigate systems that aren't designed for their achievement.

Experience with Disciplinary Measures

Too often, punitive behavior management and compliance-based techniques are used to the detriment of our learners. This is especially true for learners with divergent regulation abilities who often get pegged as a "behavior problem." This can look like learners being

> **Going Deeper with Assessments**
>
> If a caregiver, teacher, student study team, or specialist recognizes that a learner's challenges with regulation are impacting their ability to function and participate in their daily activities, then a deeper assessment may be warranted. A list of regulation assessment tools, screeners, and resources is compiled in the Appendix, page 128: Assessing Regulation Competencies.

"clipped up" or "level dropped" on a public behavior chart, sent to a seclusion space, suspended, expelled, or physically restrained—as opposed to supported with co-regulation strategies. And even more troubling is the disproportionate application of punitive measures impacting learners who are neurodivergent and/or identify as Black, Indigenous, and People of Color (BIPOC), especially boys (Nowicki, 2018 U.S. Government Accountability Office Report to Congress).

In my experience, when these disciplinary measures are used with learners with divergent regulation abilities, they fall far short of the intent to "teach them a lesson" and not exhibit a particular behavior again. Many learners have a difficult time "learning from their mistakes" because they lack the skills and abilities to do something different the next time they meet a stressor. The pain, suffering, and humiliation these learners experienced through disciplinary measures was so unsettling to me, I sought to truly teach them lessons around learning to regulate, and created The Zones to help with that quest.

In Dr. Shameka Johnson's research around this topic, she refers to this as the "school-to-prison pipeline" where we are excluding our learners from their peers starting as early as preschool, creating a path that all too often results in placement in the criminal justice system by adolescence or adulthood (2018). Her research out of Stanford University and the American Educational Research Association (AERA) correlates the vast so-called racial discipline gap with the equally vast academic achievement gap pervasive in our education system (Pearman et al., 2019). These practices based on negative behaviorism and conforming to a status-quo standard fail to foster underlying regulation skills and sever relationships, and potentially cause stress and harm for the learner.

Dr. Lori Desautels' work in educational neuroscience (*Connections Over Compliance*, 2020) redefines discipline and even consequences as "experiences." She encourages us to ask, "What experience does this learner need in order to thrive?" rather than "What consequence/disciplinary action does this learner require?" This question must come with a fundamental understanding that punitive measures frequently result in the learner feeling fear and resentment, straining the relationship with the adult. These feelings impact their sense of safety and can activate their threat detection responses. Instead, Desautels encourages providing relational, collaborative, co-regulatory experiences that build skills, foster connection, and promote regulation and learning. This in turn decreases the challenging behaviors.

Access to Supports

It may be difficult or nearly impossible for some learners and their caregivers to access the medical, therapeutic, educational, and community supports that could assist them in their regulation journey. Access can be affected by factors such as language differences, income levels, and rural vs. urban location. For example, it is estimated that less than 15% of children experiencing poverty who need mental health care are receiving it, and even fewer complete the treatment (Hodgkinson, S., Godoy, L., Beers, L.S., Lewin A., "Improving Mental Health Access for Low-Income Children and Families in the Primary Care Setting." *Pediatrics*. 2017).

Take a scenario like Miya's. She is experiencing anxiety that impacts her ability to participate in school and community events. However, no therapists who are close to public transportation accept new clients or take her family's insurance. Miya's family doesn't have a car to drive her to those therapists who do have openings and accept their insurance. Even if they find a telehealth-based therapist, covering the cost of the co-pay is another hurdle.

In other cases, families may not be aware that external support exists or feel that it is an option. Paulo's family, for example, emigrated from a country where specialists who address sensory processing and executive function were rare, and respite care and mental health wrap-around services were not part of the culture. Due to their immigration to an unfamiliar country and compounded by language barriers, Paulo's parents were unaware of access to services that could help them support Paulo's regulation differences and mental health needs.

CONCLUSION

This chapter provides a brief overview of regulation processes and various components that can impact regulation, as well as reflections you can use to help facilitate regulation in learners. If we fail to look under the hood and consider the terrain of each learner, we risk causing our learners' trauma, further dysregulating them, and even putting them at risk of becoming another statistic in the "school-to-prison pipeline." For decades we have focused on curbing behavior, perceiving learners with "challenging behavior" through a deficit lens. We need to shift our focus to developing regulation abilities, integrating strengths and lived experiences, and building a foundational skill set that will support a learner's well-being for a lifetime. To foster regulation for all, we must recognize that some of the

CHAPTER 1: Regulation from the Inside Out

> ### Zones Connection: Train with the Experts in Regulation
>
> Whether you are new to implementing a social emotional learning curriculum or looking to strengthen your expertise, Zones of Regulation trainings conveniently offer specialized live and recorded digital training for both individual and group learning. Go to zonesofregulation.com/training/ to learn more.

practices and systems that we have accepted as normal and necessary have disadvantaged and even harmed some of our learners.

The information in this chapter is not intended to be the final authority on these topics but to be enough to give you pause and whet your appetite for more learning. Hopefully, it will prompt you to consider the complexity of your learners and to better understand not only their behavior but how to support them in fostering regulation competencies going forward. It is meant to start conversations around the nature of regulation, the neuroscience it entails, and how it is impacted by one's life experiences. I encourage you to dig in and learn more by reading works by the various authors cited in this chapter, as well as the literature review and theories that have informed the development of The Zones of Regulation available at www.zonesofregulation.com. I hope this also brings insight and compassion to your work and role in creating a supportive, safe environment that allows for learning, social engagement, flourishing relationships, and regulation development. (We will continue this conversation in Chapter 3 when we examine how to build a Zones Climate to cultivate regulation.)

APPLY YOUR LEARNING

Use the following activities to apply the teachings of this chapter to promote regulation in your setting.

Reflection Question

In the What's Under the Hood and What's the Terrain sections, you learned about several factors that could impact regulation. Think about learners you have worked with who may have had regulation challenges similar to the examples in this section. Identify connections between behaviors you noticed in one of your learners and possible "under the hood" and "terrain" factors that might be related. Use the Leader Reflection Activity: Factors Impacting Regulation sheet to jot down your reflections.

Pair & Share with a Colleague

1. Identify three things you learned about regulation that could change the way you work with learners and share them with a colleague.

2. Discuss a time when you may have misinterpreted or misidentified a learner's regulation efforts based on outward behaviors. Are there "under the hood" or "terrain" factors that help you see things differently?

LEADER REFLECTION ACTIVITY: CHAPTER 1

FACTORS IMPACTING REGULATION

DIRECTIONS: Consider underlying factors that may be impacting the regulation of a learner you support. Use this reflection as a starting point for deeper exploration.

What's Under the Hood?
Neurobiological Components of Regulation

- Development
- Sensory Processing
- Executive Functioning
- Emotional Regulation
- Social Cognition
- Trauma Exposure/ACEs

What's the Terrain?
External Factors Impacting Regulation

Lived Experience • Culture • Sociopolitical Factors • Access • Relationships

Learner Name	What I observe (What the learner is expressing)	Neurobiological factors to explore	External factors to explore

THE ZONES OF REGULATION

©2024 The Zones of Regulation, Inc. All rights reserved. zonesofregulation.com

CHAPTER 2
WHAT IS THE ZONES OF REGULATION?

> **"** Using The Zones of Regulation resulted in an increase in student and teacher empathy. More positive and healthy relationships between students and teachers developed. It created a common language for all humans who enter our school. A calmer and more mindful environment ensued." **—SCHOOL ADMINISTRATOR**

> **"** Zones of Regulation has helped our whole family gain better self-awareness around how we interact with each other and our internal motivations for our actions. This has been a critical tool for keeping a peaceful home." **—CAREGIVER**

> **GOALS FOR CHAPTER**
>
> - Understand the Zones of Regulation framework, including its Signature Practices:
>   1. Categorize feelings into The Zones
>   2. Offer Zones Check-Ins
>   3. Create custom Zones Toolboxes
>   4. Use the Zones Pathway
> - Explain how Key Principles outlined support learners in learning and demonstrating regulation competencies.

OVERVIEW AND GOALS

In Chapter 1, we focused on building your understanding of regulation and the factors that impact it, including considering what's under the hood (the learner's neurobiology) and the learner's terrain (the external factors that impact regulation). Now that you have that solid foundation around the competency of regulation, let's delve into The Zones of Regulation so we have a better sense of how this framework can foster regulation. First, I'll provide an overview of The Zones of Regulation, and do a deep dive into each of the

CHAPTER 2: What Is the Zones of Regulation?

> The Zones of Regulation provides an easy way to think and communicate about how we feel on the inside by sorting our energy and emotions into four colored Zones, all of which are expected in life.

four Zones and the interceptive sensations that help to signal them. Along the way I'll highlight Signature Practices of The Zones of Regulation that contribute to learners' and leaders' success around regulation and implementing The Zones with fidelity. I end the chapter by talking about the Key Principles of The Zones of Regulation, giving you the confidence to teach The Zones values as intended.

WHAT IS THE ZONES OF REGULATION?

Feelings are complicated. They come in different sizes, intensities, and levels of energy that are unique within our brains and bodies. To make them easier to talk about, think about, and regulate, The Zones of Regulation organizes our feelings, energy levels, and internal nervous system states (also referred to as states of alertness) into the four colored categories that we call Zones.

Some feelings in the BLUE ZONE
- Bored
- Hurt
- Sick
- Tired
- Exhausted
- Sad

Low levels of energy and down feelings

Some feelings in the GREEN ZONE
- Calm
- Happy
- Okay
- Focused
- Proud
- Relaxed

Calm energy and a sense of control

Some feelings in the YELLOW ZONE
- Frustrated
- Worried
- Energetic
- Silly
- Excited
- Annoyed

Higher energy and stronger feelings

Some feelings in the RED ZONE
- Overjoyed
- Wild
- Angry
- Out of Control
- Terrified
- Furious

Extremely high energy and strongest feelings

From The Zones of Regulation Digital Curriculum (2024)

CATEGORIZE FEELINGS INTO THE ZONES
SIGNATURE PRACTICE 1

Categorizing feelings into The Zones is the first Signature Practice of The Zones of Regulation. Using the colors (blue, green, yellow, and red) to represent each Zone resonates with people across a wide range of ages and abilities by providing a common system for identifying and expressing our feeling states. By using a visual structure and vocabulary to help learners make sense of their feelings, energy, and internal states, they begin to notice that their feelings and Zones frequently change over the course of a day.

> A Zone is determined by how one feels on the inside—one's feelings, energy, and state of alertness. It is NOT determined by one's outward behavior nor the environment one is in.

Learners: Who Can Benefit?

In short, almost everyone from four-year-olds to adults! I have yet to meet a person—including myself, who has made regulation my life's work—who doesn't struggle with regulation from time to time. Though The Zones of Regulation was initially developed for neurodivergent learners with identified regulation differences—including those with autism, ADHD, mental health challenges, and cognitive disabilities—it is now used with all types and ages of learners.

Using The Zones is contagious! It doesn't just benefit the learner who is using the curriculum, it also spreads to impact and influence those who surround them—caregivers, specialist teachers, and other learners start talking about "being in the Blue Zone," "needing to use a tool," and "checking-in with my Zones." Adults who teach The Zones often report deeper insight into their own states and feelings and become more aware of the tools they can use to regulate. Many general education teachers around the globe have adopted The Zones for use with their whole class, school, and even districtwide to address their learners' social emotional learning—giving every child the chance to learn this vital life skill.

Leaders: Who Can Teach?

Anyone who works with learners ages four through adulthood can teach The Zones, including:

- General education teachers
- Special education teachers
- Occupational therapists
- Speech-language pathologists
- Psychologists
- Counselors
- Mental health practitioners
- Behaviorists
- Social workers
- Coaches
- Administrators
- Caregivers and parents

Once learners develop this self-awareness and match it to the coordinating Zone, they move on to learning how to regulate their Zones. Learners categorize which Zone, or Zones, each tool helps regulate, and explore how they can use tools to manage a Zone or move from one Zone to another. Ultimately, they create their own, individualized toolbox, and develop a cognitive pathway or mind-map to guide them in regulation. Integrating cognitive behavior therapy, learners build skills in consciously regulating their feelings and actions, manage their sensory needs, learn problem solving, and develop executive functions and social competencies.

WHY USE COLORS TO TEACH ABOUT REGULATION?

Regulation is complex, abstract, and is often done at the unconscious level, leaving adults in a position of teaching something that is difficult to explain. The Zones of Regulation solves this problem by making the complex simple, the abstract concrete, and the unconscious conscious. The real power of The Zones is its concrete visual cueing structure, four colors that each represent a Zone, which helps learners (and their co-regulators) access and organize the information they've been learning and apply it to real-time situations. Other benefits of The Zones include the following:

- Supports development of language strategies by making it easier for learners to recognize and communicate, either verbally or visually, how they are feeling in a safe, non-judgmental manner.

- Helps caregivers and leaders quickly identify how a learner feels, signaling how they may co-regulate with the learner.

- Offers an alternative way to express how one is feeling when we don't have or aren't yet ready to use words.

- Provides a common language to support positive mental health and build competencies in social emotional learning (SEL).

- Incorporates self-reflection and agency as learners explore feelings and regulation tools, and ultimately a customized toolbox of regulation supports to manage each Zone.

- Outlines a metacognitive pathway to follow, bridging self-awareness, decision-making, and active regulation.

- Supports all learners, including neurodivergent learners and those who have experienced trauma and/or who have specific goals related to their social, emotional, and behavioral development.

Overall, learners explore, sort, and apply effective regulation tools and strategies that help them manage or care for their feelings and behavior in their Zone. And at the end of the day, through using the Zones, you'll see a community develop where feelings are welcome and an openness to regulation is the norm.

THE NEUROSCIENCE BEHIND THE ZONES

While categorizing our states and feelings into four colors might seem simple at first glance, these were intentional, deliberate, and research-based in all my choices, drawing on connections to our neurophysiological states. The Zones aligns with Porges' polyvagal theory (see Chapter 1), providing learners (and adults) with a simple way to notice, understand, and ultimately respond to the state of their nervous system. See the figure below. For example, noticing one of your learners in the protective response, heightened physiological

POLYVAGAL THEORY AND ZONES OF REGULATION

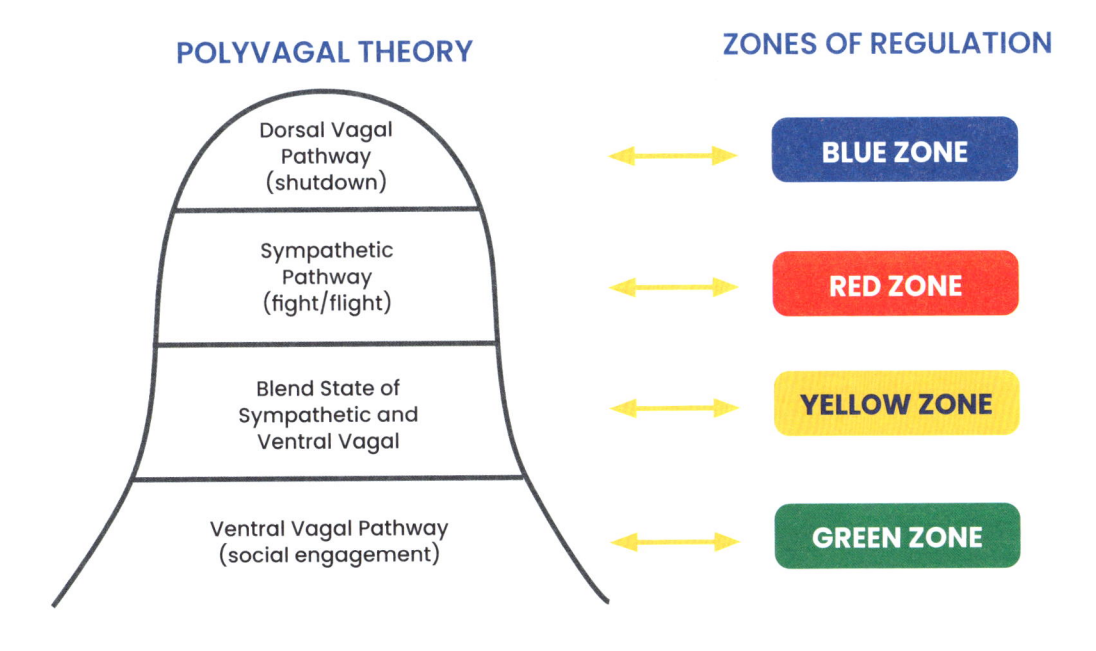

POLYVAGAL THEORY	ZONES OF REGULATION
Dorsal Vagal Pathway (shutdown)	BLUE ZONE
Sympathetic Pathway (fight/flight)	RED ZONE
Blend State of Sympathetic and Ventral Vagal	YELLOW ZONE
Ventral Vagal Pathway (social engagement)	GREEN ZONE

Katie Pagnotta, author of *Empowered by the Human Design: Utilizing the BBARS of Excellence Framework to Foster Student and Educator Success* (John Catt from Hodder Education, copyright 2024) and I co-developed this chart to show how The Zones aligns to polyvagal theory. One variance to note is how learners experience their Blue Zone: Sometimes it signifies a "shut-down" dorsal vagal response due to a threat they feel powerless against, and other times the Blue Zone will represent feelings that come with lower energy, such as sadness, discomfort, tiredness, or hurt.

(Red Zone) state versus another in a social engagement response, connected (Green Zone) state informs which learner to prioritize connecting with and gives you an idea of how to connect with that learner (with a calm, non-threatening demeanor).

This alignment can help leaders and learners, as they both notice the learner's physiological signs and signals, such as heart rate and breathing patterns, skin variations, eye pupil size, and muscle tension. This background informs how we can co-regulate, engage, and support learners. For example, when you sense a learner in the Red Zone is feeling threatened based on their external body signals, you can make sure your body language appears non-threatening and try to understand what the threat might be as you co-regulate with them.

THE FOUR ZONES SENSATIONS AND SIGNALS

Identifying what Zone (or state) we are in can be challenging, taking time and practice. Developing this awareness includes building emotional vocabulary, symbolic language, and trust in a setting or with those around us. To support this level of introspection (or awareness), The Zones of Regulation teaches the interoceptive and physiological sensations and signals commonly associated with each Zone, deepening learners' recognition and understanding of how they are feeling. This awareness is the precursor to regulation. Some of these sensations and signals are observable and MAY be clues as to the learner's physiological nervous system state and Zone. For example, slumped posture and eyes half open might indicate the body is slowing down and the learner may be in the Blue Zone, or a rigid posture or dilated eyes might indicate the body is speeding up and may be in the Red Zone. The external manifestations of these signals in learners gives us insight into what may be going on internally, helping us make sense of their behavior and be attuned to their needs. I emphasize *may* here because we are just making a best guess about the learner's feelings. For example, you notice the learner with their eyes half open and mumbling words and decide to check in with them (co-regulate). Together you discuss ideas on tools to support their Blue Zone. Each Zone and its correlating sensations and signals are explored in more detail next.

Getting Into The **Zones** of Regulation

BLUE ZONE

The Blue Zone describes low states of alertness and down feelings, such as when a person feels sad, tired, sick, hurt, lonely, or bored. Our energy is low when we are in the Blue Zone. Sometimes we identify being in the Blue Zone when our nervous system shifts to a state of "shut down" due to a threat detection or chronic stress.

Possible EXTERNAL Physiological Sensations and Signals	Possible INTERNAL Physiological Sensations and Signals
• Slumped/relaxed posture/head hung • Slow breath or sighing • Eyes heavy, tears, or staring off • Slow rate of speech • Muffled/low voice • Body moving slowly or stopped • Bottom lip out • Crying or whimpering • Mouth frowning, yawning • Weak or quiet voice	• Slow heart rate, quiet, or achy/heavy • Slow, foggy, or distracted thinking • Muscles (and/or body) feel weak/tired/limp/loose/heavy/floppy • Lump in throat • Negative self-talk (inner critic) • Low energy • Weight on chest

Bored, Hurt, Sick, Tired, Exhausted, Sad

GREEN ZONE

The Green Zone describes a calm, alert state with medium energy levels. We may be feeling comfortable, happy, focused, content, peaceful, or calm in the Green Zone. The nervous system feels safe, organized, and connected in the Green Zone, helping us be primed to learn (however, we can learn in other Zones too) and socially engage.

Possible EXTERNAL Physiological Sensations and Signals	Possible INTERNAL Physiological Sensations and Signals
• Regular or calm breath • Regular voice • Movements calm and controlled • Fidgeting/flapping	• Regular heart rate • Relaxed or regular muscles • Clear or focused thinking • Feeling comfortable • Medium energy

Calm, Happy, Okay, Focused, Proud, Relaxed

37

CHAPTER 2: What Is the Zones of Regulation?

YELLOW ZONE

The Yellow Zone describes when our energy is higher, our internal state starts to elevate, and our emotions get a little stronger. We may be experiencing stress, frustration, anxiety, excitement, silliness, confusion, overwhelm, the wiggles, or nervousness when in the Yellow Zone. (Note: The cognitive control from the upstairs brain can be accessed more easily in the Yellow Zone than in the Red Zone. Sometimes this is referred to as a blended state of the nervous system.)

TIP: Because our body and thoughts speed up in the Yellow Zone, it can be trickier to recognize and regulate while in this Zone. Learners benefit from taking extra time to explore the interoceptive signals, sensations, and triggers that relate to the Yellow Zone feelings. This awareness building helps us regulate the Yellow Zone feelings with more ease, sometimes even preventing feelings and energy to continue to build into the Red Zone, which can be more difficult to regulate.

Possible EXTERNAL Physiological Sensations and Signals

- Alert/rigid posture
- Tenser or tighter muscles
- Faster or shallow breath
- Tight jaw/clenched teeth
- Skin warm, flush cheeks/ears
- Sweaty
- Eyes wide open
- Movement: Fidgety, wiggly, faster/bigger flapping, tics
- Smiling/laughter or distressed expression (either of which can signal excitement, stress, discomfort, or anxiety)

Possible INTERNAL Physiological Sensations and Signals

- Faster or swelling heart rate
- Internal body feels warm
- Brain moving fast/difficulty focusing
- Quick, impulsive, or unfocused thoughts, or negative self-talk (inner critic)
- Fluttery or queasy/achy stomach
- Weight on chest or shoulders
- Higher energy
- Craving for, or more sensitive to, sensory input

Frustrated   Worried
Energetic   Silly
Excited   Annoyed

Getting Into The **Zones** of Regulation

RED ZONE

The Red Zone describes a state of extremely high energy and intense, overwhelming feelings that can lead us to sense a loss of control. We may be in an extremely heightened state of alertness, potentially triggering our fight, flight, freeze, or flee protective response, where our downstairs brain is on high guard and taking over to protect us (as discussed in Chapter 1). We may feel elated, euphoric, angry, rageful, devastated, out of control, panicked, or terrified when in the Red Zone.

> It is critical that we do not teach or imply that the Red Zone is "the bad Zone," rather all the Zones are expected and it is natural for all people to experience and move through the different Zones. All Red Zone feelings are valid, and some can even be comfortable and/or anticipated feelings for a situation.

Possible EXTERNAL Physiological Sensations and Signals

- Hyper alert/rigid posture
- Frozen, flopping, running, or shaking movement.
- Very tight or tense muscles and/or fists
- Rapid, shallow breath or held breath
- Eyes wide open or dilated pupils
- Clenched teeth or jaw
- Sweaty
- Flushed face/neck/chest/ears
- Goosebumps or blotchy skin
- Self-injurious behaviors
- Strong/ powerful voice

Possible INTERNAL Physiological Sensations and Signals

- Pounding or irregular/skipped heartbeat
- Hot internal body heat or chills
- Difficulty understanding, scrambled thoughts, or head is spinning
- Struggle understanding others, no sense of time, unclear memory
- Cramping or nauseous stomach
- Loss of appetite
- Body feels strong and powerful
- Inability to hear others talking
- High sensory sensitivity
- Highest energy

Overjoyed | **Wild**
Angry | **Out of Control**
Terrified | **Furious**

Numerous potential signals are listed within each Zone given the scope of emotions each encapsulates; however, in the moment of experiencing an emotion, we commonly only notice a couple of these signals. It is never expected that we feel all of these signals at once within a Zone, and not all of the signals are experienced by everyone. To help learners get in tune with their sensations and signals, they use The Zones Check-In, a Signature Practice of The Zones of Regulation framework, which is detailed in the next section.

ALL THE ZONES ARE OKAY

A core belief of The Zones of Regulation is that **all The Zones are okay.** We routinely experience a range of Zones (Blue, Green, Yellow, and possibly Red) across a day. It's critically important that we don't convey the message that the Green Zone is the only acceptable Zone to be in. If you think about it, many of us are often operating in the Yellow Zone (I know I do, feeling stressed and overwhelmed with all that I'm trying to manage). And though we are in the Yellow Zone, we are regulating; we are meeting our goals and accomplishing what needs to get done. On an ongoing basis, I encourage you to find ways to emphasize and share this message with your learners. For example, you can underscore this reality by checking in when you, personally, are in different Zones (Blue, Green, Yellow, and Red) and highlight how you are regulating them in healthy ways to be successful and support your well-being. Also, when appropriate, point out times you couldn't regulate as well, such as when you were overcome with stress in the Yellow Zone, for example, when traffic was bad and you were late to work and you realized you were so worried about getting prepared for the students, you didn't greet any of them as they walked in. Share what you would do differently next time to have a healthier outcome, such as take a couple deep breaths, remind yourself everything will work out okay, and take the moment to be present for your students as they enter. You can also use these occasions to model how to talk about the Zones. For example, "The noise in here is making me feel like I'm in the Yellow Zone and it's hard for me to think. I need to take a mindful moment to manage my Zone." Please refer to Zones Language (page 80 and in the Resources) for more insight on what to say and how to model within your setting as a Zones leader.

It is also important to recognize that for some of us, our personality and resting state may be more in the Yellow or Blue Zone than in the Green Zone. Perhaps we naturally run more energetically in the Yellow Zone or in a lower state of alertness in the Blue Zone. For example, I think of Peter, a student I worked with who identified as being in the Blue Zone most days, having low energy. Rather than making Peter feel like the Green Zone was the norm, we worked together to find strategies to help him more effectively regulate his Blue Zone so he could remain alert, attending to class and engaging with classmates. Acknowledge, accept, and support these feelings, never make anyone feel like the Green Zone is the norm.

OFFER ZONES CHECK-INS
SIGNATURE PRACTICE 2

The Zones Check-In is the second Signature Practice of The Zones of Regulation that develops the self-awareness that is foundational for regulation. A Zones Check-In starts with pausing to notice and then the following steps to tune in to our body's signals, emotions, and Zones:

- Mindfully scan your body for interoceptive **signals**.
- Get curious about your **emotions**.
- Categorize your feelings into one of the four **Zones**.

CHECK-IN BENEFITS FOR LEARNERS

Any one of these factors (body signal, emotion, Zone) may be the first thing learners notice, but they are all connected to gain self-awareness of one's feelings in a particular moment and provide an opportunity to self-monitor. The awareness that is gained through integrating this practice into daily routines sets the stage for learners to take action to regulate when needed. The simple act of pausing to check in is a valuable regulation strategy in and of itself, helping integrate the brain and body before reacting to the situation at hand. Check-ins also support communication as learners talk about or share their feelings with others and in turn receive co-regulation.

CHECK-IN BENEFITS FOR ADULTS

As adult co-regulators, a Zones Check-In gives you an opportunity to connect with learners and be attuned to their needs. For example, if you find several learners are checking in in the Yellow Zone after recess, you may dim the lighting and engage them in a brief mindfulness exercise before jumping into the academics. Taking a moment to connect with a learner who checks in in the Red Zone can potentially steer them in a very different direction than if you didn't have that information only to see that learner melt down with unsafe behavior. We can use a Zones Check-In as our first line of support, rather than

CHAPTER 2: What Is the Zones of Regulation?

starting with a behavior correction or redirection. This "feelings first" approach can have a positive impact on relationships and the climate of a home, classroom, or other setting.

It is important to know that you should never force a learner to check in. Some learners will want more privacy around this, which is fine, while others will feel comfortable sharing. Honor where each learner's comfort level is, which may mean forgoing having a learner check-in or offering an alternative way to do it. I'll go into more detail about Zones Check-Ins and their impact on climate in the next chapter.

REGULATING OUR ZONES WITH TOOLS

Regulation tools help our brain and body, via our nervous system, work together to manage our feelings, energy, thoughts, and behavior. Some tools work as a bottom-up approach (from body to brain), helping us process and integrate our senses through sensory-motor activity or inputs, such as wall-pushes, going for a walk, or smelling something soothing. Others work as a top-down approach (from brain to body), helping us organize our thinking or cognition in order to support a healthy mind and body. Regulation tools and strategies explored in the curriculum include:

- Sensory and motor tools
- Mind and body tools
- Thinking and planning tools
- Connecting tools

The Zones of Regulation framework helps not only organize our feelings, but also organize our tools, making regulation easier for us. Because each Zone encompasses distinct levels of energy, states, and emotions, how we regulate them differs. For example, a tool that helps us regulate in the Red Zone to feel safe and in control is often not as helpful in the Blue Zone when we need to energize.

Tools will look and feel different for each of us, depending on our physiology, culture, identity, and lived experience. In the curriculum, we explore a variety of regulation tools, allowing learners to gravitate toward the tools that have the most impact on their systems.

MORE ZONES RESOURCES
Tools to Try Cards

The *Zones Tools to Try Cards for Kids* (ages 5–10) and *Tools to Try for Tweens & Teens* (ages 10+) sets include over fifty 4"× 6" tool cards. These two separate decks are an easy, user-friendly way to introduce regulation strategies and empower learners to choose tools that work best for them. Each strategy card displays the regulation tool on one side and a how-to-do-it description on the reverse, along with a metacognitive self-reflection.

REGULATING THE BLUE ZONE >>

Our Blue Zone tools help us energize, rest, or gain comfort. When we are in the Blue Zone, we regulate by seeking (or co-regulate by offering) comfort, energizing, or resting. If we are feeling sick in the Blue Zone, we may need to rest. If we are feeling tired, we may need to energize or re-charge, depending on the situation. If we are feeling sad, we may need comfort. In all these situations, the common theme is noticing our lower energy and/or down feelings and options for managing them.

REGULATING THE GREEN ZONE >>

Our Green Zone tools help us feel well, healthy, and focused. They can also help us adjust our energy if we need to rev up or power down to be successful in our pursuit. In the Green Zone, we might regulate by choosing to eat a healthy snack, exercise, take a break, or pause for a mindful moment. These restorative action tools help us proactively care for ourselves so we can be in an optimal state to take on what's ahead.

It is important that when we teach The Zones, we do not emphasize "getting back to the Green Zone" or reward learners for being in the Green Zone. This undermines the core principle that all The Zones are okay. In fact, sometimes you may need to regulate your Green Zone to meet your goal. For example, trying to compete in a soccer game while feeling calm in the Green Zone might require you to regulate by working to rev your energy up so you can play more aggressively against your opponents to win. Another example is being lost in a good book at bedtime, feeling content and focused in the Green Zone, yet you want to wind down in order to meet your goal of getting enough sleep.

> **TIP:** It's often easy to overlook providing access and the opportunity to use tools that support regulation of the Green Zone because our systems are feeling comfortable already; however, it is key to proactively provide meaningful inputs such as movement opportunities, screen breaks, drinking water—things that keep our bodies feeling regulated, safe, connected, and organized. This is especially true for learners with sensory differences, a history of trauma, and/or adverse childhood experiences (ACEs) who may be more prone to move quickly between Zones. Customizing the Green Zone toolbox with lots of proactive tools can help support the organization of the nervous system that correlates with Green Zone feelings.

BLUE ZONE TOOLS
Provide energy, comfort, or rest.

GREEN ZONE TOOLS
Help us feel well, healthy, alert, or focused.

CHAPTER 2: What Is the Zones of Regulation?

YELLOW ZONE TOOLS
Help us slow down and feel in control and calmer.

RED ZONE TOOLS
Help us pause and feel calmer, safer, and more in control.

«« REGULATING THE YELLOW ZONE

While in the Yellow Zone, our energy and feelings are not as strong as in the Red Zone but are still a bit elevated, so regulation often helps us slow down or be cautious. Our Yellow Zone tools help us calm our energy and strengthen the communication between our upstairs and downstairs brains so we can reestablish a sense of control. For example, if we are feeling energetic at the lunch table, it helps to use caution and take a deep breath so we do not spill something. If we are feeling nervous before our performance, we can slow down our racing thoughts and speech by using a mindfulness tool. When we are frustrated, we can take a break to collect ourselves before we say or do something we regret.

«« REGULATING THE RED ZONE

We can regulate the Red Zone by pausing to gain control of our big feelings or releasing some energy to feel calmer. Our Red Zone tools are our most powerful tools. In fact, we might even refer to them as our "power tools." They help us feel calmer, safer, and more in control, giving us the chance to pause or stop ourselves before we act upon our impulse. For example, if we are feeling angry it may help to walk away. If we are panicked, we use our self-talk to tell us to "stop and think" and help us gain a sense of control of our thoughts and actions in order to meet our goal. If we are elated, such as when a teammate scores the winning point, we might need to pause and take a big breath to regulate our impulse to run out on the field to celebrate if there is still time on the clock.

> **TIP:** It is important to note that although the strong signals associated with the Red Zone make it easier for some to identify when we are in the Red Zone vs. the Yellow Zone, it's often the hardest Zone for us to manage because the big feelings from the downstairs brain can overwhelm and shut down our thinking abilities in the upstairs brain. It takes more time and practice to learn how to regulate our Red Zone. Even as adults, we sometimes struggle to regulate our Red Zone feelings.

CREATE CUSTOM ZONES TOOLBOXES
SIGNATURE PRACTICE 3

In the Zones curriculum, after practicing and exploring a variety of tools, each learner reflects on how a tool helps or affects them, and ultimately creates a custom Zones Toolbox of preferred and effective tools for each Zone. This third Signature Practice of The Zones of Regulation supports learners in building self-efficacy so they can learn to notice, express, and ultimately determine how best to regulate their feelings, states, and energy. The visual, color-coded structure of the Zones Toolboxes serves as a menu or visual representation of regulation strategies to choose from, easing access and decreasing the need for auditory cueing from adults. Having customized toolboxes creates an inclusive and equitable climate where all can regulate based upon what they need.

It is important to note that we don't always need tools to regulate our Zones; however, they are helpful when we need to regulate to accomplish our goals, complete a task, or want to change our feelings and support our well-being. Often a learner might check in in a Zone, such as feeling excited in the Yellow Zone, and report, "I can handle/manage it." If they are accomplishing what they need/want to do, then that is fantastic. However, if their dysregulation is hindering them from success, it might be helpful to ask them about their goals, or state the expectation, and gently encourage them to take a look at their Yellow Zone toolbox to see if a tool might help. We will be discussing use of tools and our Zones Toolbox in the next chapter on Zones Climate.

TOOL TIPS

1. **Modeling matters.** Demonstrating and reflecting on using tools as an adult is incredibly impactful for learners. You can use phrases such as: *"I'm going to pause and use a tool before we start our activity,"* or *"I'm feeling really sleepy. I'm going to use one of my Blue Zone tools and drink some water,"* or *"I was really frustrated about [fill in the blank] yesterday and needed to take some deep breaths to be able to manage my Yellow Zone."*

2. **Regulation tools are for well-being, not compliance.** We do not encourage using tools for behavior management or as a compliance technique, although being in control of one's behavior is often a by-product of using a tool effectively.

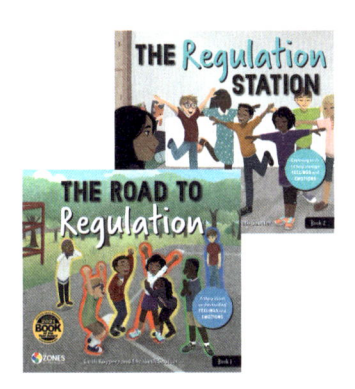

MORE ZONES RESOURCES
Zones Storybook Set

These two award-winning storybooks engage children ages 5–11 in learning The Zones of Regulation framework and curriculum. The first, *The Road to Regulation,* describes and explains four different emotional Zones and how we feel in each one of them. Through an imaginary adventure to *The Regulation Station,* the second storybook introduces the use of regulation tools to help learners identify ways they can manage their different feelings. Learn more at www.socialthinking.com.

CHAPTER 2: What Is the Zones of Regulation?

3. **Empower learners to explore and determine which tools work for them.** Tools are not "one size fits all." They will differ from person to person and from Zone to Zone. Part of gaining independence in regulation is trying out new tools over time, and reflecting on which ones help toward goals, jobs/tasks, and well-being.

4. **Teach tools with intention.** Taking a thorough approach to modeling and practicing a wide variety of tools within your setting will set your learners up for success.

5. **Tools are a choice, not a mandate.** Always provide the option to use a tool without forcing it. This will encourage learners to develop agency in regulation.

6. **Tools vs. toys.** Many new tools or techniques have a "novelty effect" that will diminish over time. Thoroughly model how to effectively use a particular tool, allow opportunities to explore the tool, and help learners notice when it is interfering with their ability to meet their goals.

7. **Acknowledge when learners make an attempt to "try" a tool**, even if it doesn't work well in the moment. It is likely a step in the right direction to building regulation skills.

8. **Teach tools over time.** We encourage you to continue introducing and practicing new tools while also revisiting previously taught tools to keep them in the front of mind.

USE THE ZONES PATHWAY
SIGNATURE PRACTICE 4

After our learners are familiar with the Zones and have established their toolboxes, we introduce the fourth Signature Practice of The Zones of Regulation, the Zones of Regulation Pathway. The Zones Pathway builds upon concepts introduced throughout the curriculum that provide learners with more scaffolding to apply what they learned about the four Zones and their related tools in real-time situations. In the Zones Pathway, we walk through a process to notice our situation, identify our feelings, and to make healthy decisions about managing them. It's not just about how we feel, but how we care for our feelings and behaviors so we have a sense of well-being, can meet our goals, and do our job (task demands). To make this process as easy to follow as possible, the Zones of Regulation Pathway includes 5 concrete steps that learners and

MORE ZONES RESOURCES
Navigating The Zones (ages 8+)

This unique and fun cooperative game expands the teachings of *The Zones of Regulation® Digital Curriculum*. It introduces the concept of the Zones Pathway via a board game that encourages interaction by using a variety of card decks to explore social situations, emotions, and related regulation tools. Learners collaborate as they practice problem solving how to navigate the regulation of the four Zones. Learners should already have a strong working knowledge of The Zones of Regulation concepts and vocabulary.

Getting Into The **Zones** of Regulation

THE ZONES OF REGULATION PATHWAY

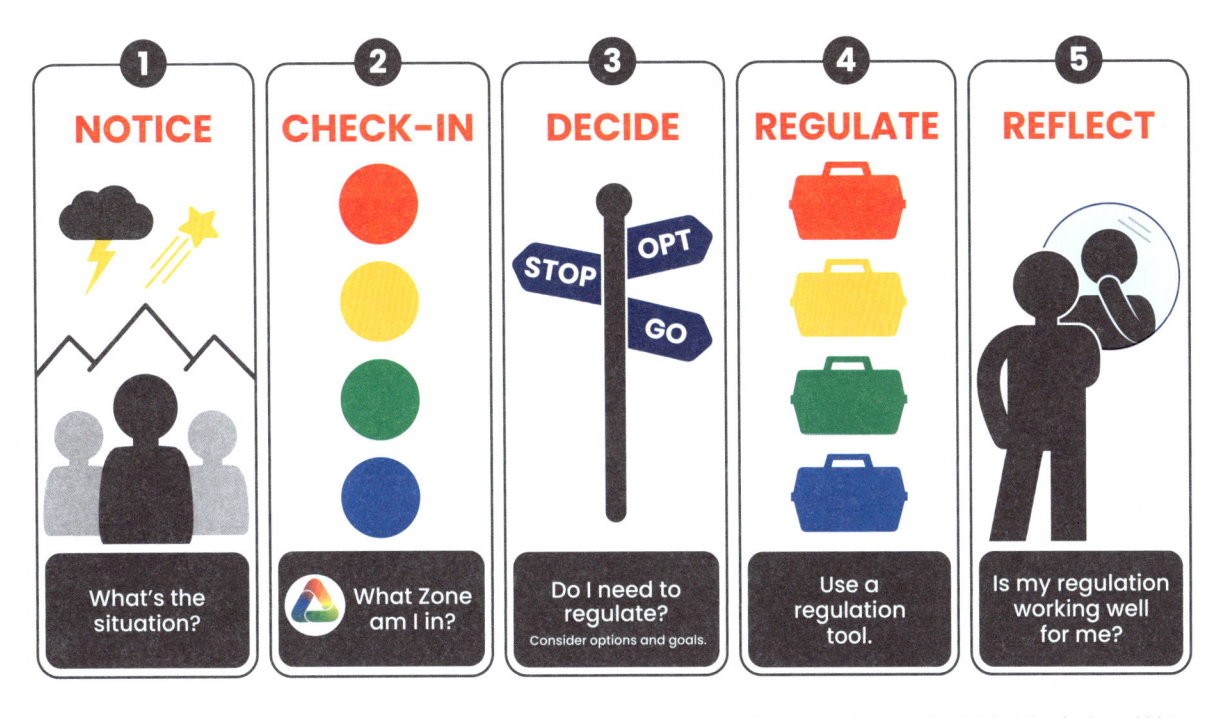

1 NOTICE — What's the situation?

2 CHECK-IN — What Zone am I in?

3 DECIDE — Do I need to regulate? Consider options and goals.

4 REGULATE — Use a regulation tool.

5 REFLECT — Is my regulation working well for me?

Source: The Zones of Regulation Digital Curriculum, 2024

their co-regulators can follow. Once we introduce the pathway in the curriculum, we continue to revisit it, providing many opportunities for learners to practice the steps so they become more routine. Review the graphic and examples on the next spread before continuing.

PATHWAY VARIABLES

The Zones of Regulation Pathway provides a consistent, systematic process to consciously regulate while also allowing for all the natural variables in life. The combination of triggers/sparks, context, climate (which we will discuss in Chapter 3), feelings, Zones, and tools will differ, but the 5 steps of the pathway remain the same. For example, let's shift the context from the example (on pages 48/49) to you: You are alone in your bedroom and receive a text that you did not get a part in the play. In this scenario, you have the same trigger, not getting a part, but now in a different setting (step 1). You have the same feeling of devastation in the Red Zone (step 2), but because the context differs, you don't have the social goal of maintaining positive

Continued on page 50

**MORE ZONES RESOURCES:
Triggers and Sparks Poster**

Use this 24" × 18" dry-erase poster to brainstorm triggers and sparks with your learners.

THE ZONES PATHWAY IN ACTION

STEP 1: NOTICE

GUIDING QUESTIONS: What's the situation? Was there a trigger or spark?

KEY VOCABULARY AND CONCEPTS

- **SITUATION:** What is happening at a certain time and place.
- **TRIGGER:** An unwelcome situation that causes us to feel less regulated.
- **SPARK:** A welcome situation that causes us to feel less regulated.

EXAMPLE: You are a 13-year-old learner transitioning in the hallway between classes, surrounded by many peers and teachers (situation). On the bulletin board, you see a posting of who got a part in the school play. You look for your name, but it isn't on the list. Bad news delivered in this public way is a trigger for you (though if you had gotten the part, it would have been a spark for you).

STEP 2: CHECK-IN

GUIDING QUESTION: What Zone am I in?

KEY VOCABULARY AND CONCEPTS

- **ZONES CHECK-IN:** Pausing to notice and identify how we feel. This self-awareness includes thinking about our:
  - **BODY SIGNALS:** The sensations inside our bodies that help us figure out how we feel (interoception)
  - **EMOTIONS:** Feelings we have.
  - **ZONE:** A category used to describe our feelings on the INSIDE (which includes emotions, energy, and alertness)

EXAMPLE: You notice your heart begins to race, your muscles tense and feel powerful, and your skin gets hot. Checking-in, you identify feeling devastated in the Red Zone.

STEP 3: DECIDE

GUIDING QUESTION: Do I need to regulate?

KEY VOCABULARY AND CONCEPTS

- **REGULATE:** To adjust, manage, or control something so it works well. This includes considering our goals, jobs or tasks, and well-being.
- **GOALS:** Something we work toward to accomplish or achieve. We can think of things we are working toward over time as *Later Goals* (such as getting a good grade at the end of the quarter or graduating from high school) and things we are working toward in the present moment as *Now Goals* (such as having fun, being safe, following a rule, completing a task).
- **OPTIONS:** Choices we have (in a situation). (In this step we answer the question, "Do I need to regulate with a tool?" We consider our options and how each may or may not help us reach our goal.)

EXAMPLE: With everyone around you, your goal is to "keep it together" in the middle of the hall. You consider your options and how they may work out for you:

1. Swearing and bolting out of the school would likely cause me to be in trouble.
2. Marching up to confront the drama teacher would not likely change the outcome.
3. Going to the bathroom for some privacy and taking some deep breaths to regulate.

Using the Stop, Opt & Go strategy, you choose Option 3, deciding this will help you gain more control of your Red Zone feelings before going to class.

Getting Into The **Zones** of Regulation

STEP 4: REGULATE

TAKE ACTION: Use a regulation tool.

KEY VOCABULARY AND CONCEPTS

- **REGULATION TOOL:** A strategy, or something we do, to manage our Zones.
- **ZONES TOOLBOX:** A collection of regulation tools for each Zone.

EXAMPLE: You head to the bathroom, knowing a quieter space will be helpful. You use a Red Zone tool from your toolbox—deep breathing. You continue to breathe as the stress in your body unwinds. You begin to notice your heartbeat slowing down and sense you are gaining more control of your feelings and actions.

STEP 5: REFLECT

GUIDING QUESTION: Is my regulation working well for me?

KEY VOCABULARY AND CONCEPTS

- **OUTCOME:** The result of something.
- **REFLECT:** To carefully think about something.
- **WELL-BEING:** Feeling well, healthy, comfortable, and/or successful.

In this step, you may consider the following questions:

- Am I accomplishing my goals?
- Can I do the task or job I need to?
- How are my health and well-being?
- Do I need to revisit the pathway?

Sometimes our tools work well, other times they don't. Maybe we didn't think we needed to regulate at step 3, but now realize we might. If you find that you aren't managing your Zone as well as you wanted, you can go through the Zones Pathway again. Otherwise, you are likely ready to move on with your day.

EXAMPLE: Using your Red Zone tools helped you gain control of Red Zone feelings and regulate your reactions to meet your goals. However, you notice you are now feeling disappointed and in the Blue Zone about not getting the part. Revisiting the pathway, you use a Blue Zone tool—self-talk—to remind yourself, "it is what it is" and accept it. Regulating your Red Zone (and now your Blue Zone) has allowed you to gain a sense of well-being and feel ready enough to join your class. You met your goals of maintaining positive relations with your peers and teachers and avoided any negative outcomes.

NOTE: All of us are entitled to our feelings and it is expected that we all experience Red Zone feelings. The key take-away is that we all recognize our Red Zone feelings and take steps to regulate them when needed, managing our actions in a way that allows us to meet our goals, and care for our feelings in a safe and healthy way that supports our well-being. You may still feel upset, yet are managing your feelings and actions in a way that is adaptive to the situation around you.

CHAPTER 2: What Is the Zones of Regulation?

BODY SIGNALS: The sensations inside our body that help us figure out how we feel (interoception).

EMOTIONS: Feelings we have.

GOALS: Something we work toward to accomplish or achieve. We can think of things we are working toward over time as Later Goals (such as getting a good grade at the end of the quarter or graduating from high school) and things we are working toward in the present moment as Now Goals (such as having fun, being safe, solving a problem, finishing a job or task).

OPTIONS: Choices we have in a situation.

OUTCOME: The result of something.

REFLECT: To carefully think about something.

REGULATE: To adjust, manage, or control something so it works well. This includes considering our goals, jobs or tasks, and well-being.

REGULATION TOOL: A strategy, or something we do, to manage our Zones.

SITUATION: What is happening at a certain time and place, including the people around us.

Continued from page 47

relations with those around you and avoiding school consequences. Therefore, regulation looks different, and you opt not to use a Red Zone tool to manage your Zone (step 3). Instead, you curse out loud and slam your fist down on your bed (step 4) and find yourself feeling better after letting out some steam (step 5). Again, even though the variables changed, you followed the 5 steps.

KEY PRINCIPLES OF THE ZONES OF REGULATION

Along with the Signature Practices associated with The Zones that are outlined earlier in this chapter, I want to emphasize and reinforce the following Key Principles around The Zones of Regulation framework. To ensure that The Zones curriculum is implemented with fidelity, we need to embrace each of these values:

- **Zones are based on feelings, not behaviors.** Let's take behavior out of this equation. We determine our Zones based on our feelings, our energy, and our internal state of alertness. Our behavior does not necessarily indicate or reflect our feelings (or Zone). Behaviors can sometimes help give us (and the learners) clues as to what Zone a learner may be in, but the important focus needs to be on the factors underlying the behavior in order to properly support the learner in the moment. And behaviors are *impacted* by how we *manage* our Zone (or feelings). When we are able to use our tools and regulate our Zone, we are in turn regulating our behaviors to be adaptive for the situation.

- **All The Zones are okay, and we really mean this.** Remembering that our Zone is based on our feelings, it's okay to be in the Yellow Zone when you feel wiggly or full of energy after recess or irritated if your clothes just aren't feeling quite right. It's okay to come into the classroom in the Blue Zone, feeling tired or let down. It's okay to be furious in the Red Zone when you feel bullied, or panicked when your body feels bombarded with sensory stimulation. Feelings and fluctuations in our energy and internal states are innate, and it is human nature to experience a wide range of feelings; this is something we all are entitled to and is integral to how we teach The Zones of Regulation. With this self-awareness, we can explore healthy and adaptive tools to help us regulate our goals, tasks, and well-being.

- **Our experience of The Zones is unique.** Each of us experiences our feelings in our own, unique way. Building self-awareness of feelings and giving learners the opportunity to relate them to each Zone allows for individuality. For example, some people may experience boredom as stressful and associate it with the Yellow Zone, whereas others experience it as a quiet, withdrawn feeling and relate it to the Blue Zone. Also, we can identify in more than one Zone at a time as we can experience more than one feeling at a time, such as feeling tired in the Blue Zone and nervous for a test in the Yellow Zone.

- **The Zones of Regulation is not a compliance-based model. Period.** It is a proactive teaching approach that builds awareness of the unique feelings we each have, gives us a common language for connecting and communicating these feelings, and provides us practice with tools and strategies to take care of ourselves. Any model in which learners are rewarded or praised for being in the Green Zone, or shamed for being in the Red, Yellow, or Blue Zone is a misrepresentation of The Zones of Regulation.

- **The Green Zone is not the goal.** As adults often co-regulating with learners, we can support them in regulating their feelings and Zones with compassion, free of expectations or contingencies for being in, or returning to, the Green Zone. While the Green Zone often gives us a feeling of comfort, calm, and connectedness inside of our bodies, use of The Zones in your setting should not project any value of the Green Zone above the other colored Zones. We have evolved our language to say, *"Let's use a tool to help us care for/manage/regulate our Zone,"* to ensure learners don't feel pressure to be in the Green Zone.

> **SPARK:** A welcome situation that causes us to feel less regulated.
>
> **TRIGGER:** An unwelcome situation that causes us to feel less regulated.
>
> **WELL-BEING:** Feeling well, healthy, comfortable, and/or successful.
>
> **ZONE:** A category used to describe our feelings on the INSIDE (including emotions and energy).
>
> **ZONES CHECK-IN:** Pausing to notice and identify how we feel. This self-awareness includes thinking about our body's signals, emotions, and Zone.
>
> **ZONES TOOLBOX:** A collection of regulation tools for each Zone.

CONCLUSION

The Zones of Regulation is so much more than posting visuals of the four Zones and feelings associated with them. The Zones of Regulation framework outlined in this chapter, along with the four Signature Practices (1. Categorize feelings into The Zones; 2. Offer Zones Check-Ins; 3. Create custom Zones Toolboxes; 4. Use the Zones Pathway) that are taught in the Digital Curriculum, build in complexity, developing learners' understanding and ability to regulate, as they move through the following skills:

CHAPTER 2: What Is the Zones of Regulation?

- Recognizing a broader range of emotions in others and in self
- Noticing their body signals and sensations (interoception)
- Understanding the context of the situation
- Gaining insight into events that cause them to change Zones (referred to as triggers and sparks)
- Inhibiting impulses and problem solving positive outcomes
- Learning when and how to use regulation tools
- Understanding why regulation matters in relation to their overall wellness and personal goals
- Following a pathway to sequence the regulation process

Using The Zones of Regulation and adhering to its Key Principles embeds each learner's unique physiology and preferences in the regulation process, providing them agency to regulate in a way that works for them and honors their sense of self. In addition, The Zones of Regulation provides a system to support co-regulation that helps leaders not only recognize where their learners are physiologically and emotionally within the four Zones, but that also guides their interactions (e.g., communication style, body language, modification of demands) and the supports they offer. Now that we understand the foundational concepts of The Zones of Regulation, we next explore how to create a Zones Climate that incorporates these Signature Practices while also promoting safety and respect, and allowing regulation to flourish.

APPLY YOUR LEARNING

Use the following activities to process what you learned in this chapter regarding the fundamentals of The Zones of Regulation.

Reflection Questions

1. In the overview of the four Zones, you learned about possible sensations and signals for each of the Zones. Reflect on how you experience the different Zones by completing the Leader Reflection Activity: My Zones and Signals sheet on page 54. List a common feeling you experience along with your associated sensations and signals for each Zone.

2. In the Zones of Regulation Pathway section, you learned about the 5 steps to regulation. Use the Leader Reflection Activity: My Zones Pathway Reflection sheet (on page 55) to reflect on a recent experience you had in which you successfully used

MORE ZONES RESOURCES:
Pathway Posters

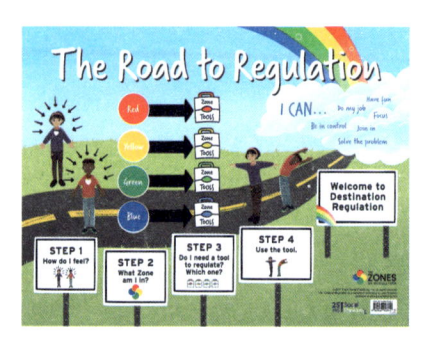

The Road to Regulation Poster

Adapted from the colorful 2-page layout in *The Regulation Station* storybook, this 24" × 18" poster summarizes the Zones of Regulation Pathway and the lessons taught throughout The Zones of Regulation 2-Storybook Set.

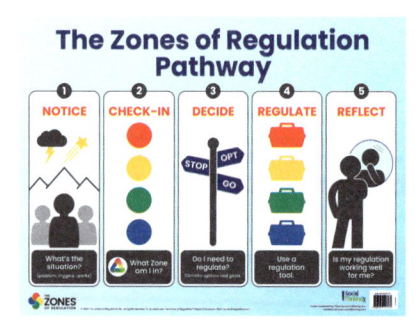

The Zones of Regulation Pathway Poster

This 24" × 18" poster encapsulates the learning in *The Zones of Regulation Digital Curriculum*, creating easy-to-follow actionable steps to support learners through the regulation process.

a tool/strategy to regulate yourself. Identify how you used (or could have used) the 5 steps to manage your feelings and behaviors during this experience. Change variables along the pathway to explore different possibilities, including shifting the context of the setting and opting to regulate or not.

Pair & Share with a Colleague

- Compare and contrast the sensations and signals you identified for each of the Zones in Reflection Question 1.

- To explore the concept "All The Zones Are Okay," keep note of how you move through The Zones over the course of a day. How many Zones were you in, and how many times per Zone? Share your findings with a colleague.

- Share your pathway example from Question 2 in the Reflection Questions section with a colleague. Discuss how reflecting on how we as leaders experience the pathway can help us teach the concepts to learners.

- Discuss the Key Principles of The Zones of Regulation with a colleague or caregiver. Identify which principle might be hardest for you to fully embrace and why. Together, brainstorm strategies you can use to ensure you embrace all the principles.

LEADER REFLECTION ACTIVITY: CHAPTER 2

MY ZONES AND SIGNALS

DIRECTIONS: In the space below, list common emotions you experience in each Zone, as well as the signals and sensations that you associate with it.

BLUE ZONE
Low levels of energy and down feelings

Emotion	Sensation/Signal

GREEN ZONE
Calm energy and a sense of control

Emotion	Sensation/Signal

YELLOW ZONE
Higher energy and stronger feelings

Emotion	Sensation/Signal

RED ZONE
Extremely high energy and our strongest feelings

Emotion	Sensation/Signal

LEADER REFLECTION ACTIVITY: CHAPTER 2

MY ZONES PATHWAY REFLECTION

DIRECTIONS: Reflect on how you have experienced *The Zones of Regulation* Pathway by completing the steps below for a recent event.

STEP 1: NOTICE
What's a recent situation? Was there a trigger or spark?

_____
_____
_____

STEP 2: CHECK-IN
What Zone were you in?

_____
_____
_____

STEP 3: DECIDE
Did you need to regulate? Consider your options and goals.

_____
_____
_____

STEP 4: REGULATE
What did this look like to you? Describe using your chosen tool.

_____
_____
_____

STEP 5: REFLECT
Did your regulation work well for you? Consider your goals and well-being.

_____
_____

Is there anything you would have done differently?

_____
_____

THE ZONES OF REGULATION

©2024 The Zones of Regulation, Inc. All rights reserved. zonesofregulation.com

55

CHAPTER 3
BUILDING THE ZONES CLIMATE

OVERVIEW AND GOALS

What is "climate"? The climate, or culture, of a setting or environment can be thought of as how someone experiences and feels in that space (be it a school, home, or therapeutic group). The climate can have a profound impact on the social and emotional functioning, mental health, and achievement of the people in that setting; we can feel safe, secure, and comfortable there, or the opposite—insecure or in danger. Norms, values, interpersonal relationships, and past experiences all impact the climate. By implementing *The Zones* with fidelity, we build a climate that fosters a sense of safety, belonging, respect, inclusion, and connection.

The Zones Climate is a series of best practices that, when integrated together, create an environment that values and nurtures well-being. The Zones Climate is how we bring the values and concepts in *The Zones of Regulation® Digital Curriculum* to life, offering leaders and learners safe spaces to learn about and practice skills and competencies for regulation and well-being. We build the Zones Climate not only through the instruction and co-regulation support we provide to our learners, but also through exhibiting our own social emotional competencies. The practices and considerations explored in this chapter can and should be used anywhere The Zones is taught or integrated, including school, home, clinical, and community settings.

> **GOALS FOR CHAPTER**
> - Reflect on actions you can take to build a climate of well-being for learners.
> - Apply the Essential Elements of the Zones Climate in your setting to promote a foundation for regulation to flourish.

CHAPTER 3: Building the Zones Climate

BENEFITS OF THE ZONES CLIMATE

All too often, the cultural and institutional systems where we live, learn, and work have climates that are built for "typical" learners; they emphasize compliance and adherence to social norms that don't apply to all the learners. Historically, learners with divergent regulation abilities have endured seclusion, overidentification for special education, and a disproportionate number of punitive measures within school settings and beyond into community life. For example, in schools, divergent learners often need to leave their primary peer settings (i.e., their classroom) to receive regulation support, rather than having these supports addressed and integrated into their familiar classroom. The Zones of Regulation helps address this problem by building a climate that centers on well-being and fosters inclusion within environments for those across the diversity spectrum including (but not limited to) neurodiversity, racial and cultural diversity, language diversity, gender diversity, and those with trauma exposures.

Here are ways that The Zones of Regulation benefits and empowers both learners and leaders:

- Provides a neutral common language—free from cultural bias—to communicate about feelings.

- Places value on internal/emotional state vs. outward behavior.

- Shifts focus and discussion among adults from a behavior management lens (What's the problem we need to stop?) to a social/emotional skill development lens (What skills might the learner need and how can I support their development?).

- Fosters emotional equality between leaders and learners; we all experience all the Zones and are all actively working on regulation in our daily lives.

- Honors learners' voices by giving them an opportunity and means to authentically express their internal states and feelings.

- Increases learners' agency by exploring a variety of regulation tools and strategies they can opt to use, plus allows for time, space, and opportunities to practice them.

- Reduces the need for learners to leave their environment to regulate and the stigma associated with that, thereby increasing instructional time and inclusion with peers.

- Develops empathy and understanding for those who need more support with regulation skills; seeing them as learners who are working on developing skills rather than as kids with "behavior problems," "anger issues," etc.

- Enables access and support for learners at all stages of skill development on the continuum of regulation skills, from co-regulation to self-regulation.

- Provides a simple framework and common language around feelings and emotions to communicate with families, caregivers, and other supportive adults to effectively partner and collaborate in supporting the social emotional well-being for all learners.

You can reap these benefits in your setting by taking the actions and implementing the Essential Elements described in this chapter.

BUILDING THE FOUNDATION FOR REGULATION: TAKING ACTION

No matter your role, every one of us can significantly impact learners' lives and contribute to the climate—sometimes without even realizing it! We can set the stage for learners to flourish and have a smoother journey ahead through how we both "talk the talk" and "walk the walk." Now, let's identify responsibilities you have as a Zones leader.

1. REGULATE YOURSELF

I like to think about how we adults regulate as an anchor versus a catapult, where we have the power to transform the emotions of the learners around us. This can be for the positive or negative depending on how we regulate ourselves. Emotions are contagious and the ripple effects can be vast. No doubt your role as a caregiver, educator, or therapist can be trying and sometimes cause feelings of worry, frustration, and anger. However, our learners are watching and their systems are firing. Wouldn't you rather be the anchor that steadies them rather than the catapult that launches them into dysregulation? Mona Delahooke suggests that when we offer a calm, warm, inviting presence, our learners' nervous systems will be less on guard, providing them that internal sense of safety (2019).

> "To help children build their emotional intelligence and resilience, we must simultaneously tend to our own emotional intelligence and resilience." —ELENA AGUILAR

When we sense our own dysregulation, we can acknowledge our feelings and find healthy ways to regulate them. Not only will we be modeling for our learners, but we will also be setting the tone

CHAPTER 3: Building the Zones Climate

that it is natural that we all work hard to regulate. This is referred to as "therapeutic use of self," and through this self-disclosure, relationships can be strengthened, and learners sense a balance of power—the adults are working on regulation too. In fact, over the years, many caregivers and educators have told me that The Zones of Regulation lessons are also beneficial for them.

As adults, many of us don't have enough time to practice, cultivate, and attend to our own well-being, let alone that of others. Think of it like this: When you're flying, you put on the oxygen mask and take care of yourself before you help the child with theirs. The same holds true for regulation. We must engage in our own self-care and regulation first, putting us in a better position to help others by providing that safe space for them to work through their feelings. We also need to acknowledge that despite our best efforts, we will become dysregulated and make mistakes. Use these opportunities to model self-compassion and a growth mindset. When we have a learner who is persistently shouting out during class discussions and we become dysregulated by raising our voice and saying, "How many times have I told you to raise your hand?!" we are not helping the learner and might even be shaming them. If we react this way, first use self-compassion and remember that we are imperfect beings. Then, start to repair by saying, "I shouldn't have said that. I ignored my body signals, and I wish I had used my deep-breathing tool before I said anything to you." This models to all that you acknowledge your mistake and shows how the situation can be repaired. Then, it's important to circle back with that learner and provide an opportunity for them to express any feelings they have about what happened. "I want you to know that it's okay for you to be upset with me. You are welcome to let me know that. I will understand and I won't be upset. You have a right to your feelings."

As we grow in our understanding of regulation, we can improve our own regulation skills and become more effective co-regulators with others. Here are some ways to re-boot your regulation journey.

Think About:

- Patterns in my own regulation: Are there certain times of day when I need to consistently attend to my regulation?

- Triggers in my environment that cause dysregulated feelings, such as stress, irritation, exhaustion, worry.

> When you're flying, you put on the oxygen mask and take care of yourself before you help the child with theirs. The same holds true for regulation. We must engage in our own self-care and regulation first, putting us in a better position to help others by providing that safe space for them to work through their feelings.

- How is my body reacting to stressors? Am I modeling a safe, connected, calm state to help others' nervous systems be less on guard?

- What tools help when I am feeling dysregulated?

- Do I need to regulate myself so I can be available to co-regulate with the learner?

Actions/Strategies:

- Communicate how you are feeling and your regulation strategies to learners, normalizing how everyone experiences a range of feelings and works on regulation.

- Schedule proactive use of wellness tools into your day.

- Have your own personal Zones Toolbox that is easily accessible.

- Set up systems with other supportive adults so you can "tag out" when you need to use a regulation tool. This can be a co-parent, neighboring teacher, or teaching assistant, etc.

- Repair with others when necessary, to model taking accountability for one's mistakes.

2. BUILD RELATIONSHIPS

Relationships built on trust and compassion are at the heart of what we do. I have seen time and again how a relationship can impact the trajectory for learners from all walks of life. When learners feel connected to you and are seen, respected, and feel safe, they are more likely to take on the learning challenges you ask of them. In addition, Alexs Pate, author of *The Innocent Classroom* (2020), suggests that building authentic relationships with learners can help dismantle racism, stereotypes, and biases in our schools. Through relationships with our learners, Pate says we establish trust and preserve a child's innocence and goodness, allowing each learner to experience a full range of emotions because they know the adults are still going to be by their side even if they don't always manage those feelings in optimal ways.

> "I've learned that people will forget what you said, people will forget what you did, but people will never forget how you made them feel."
> —MAYA ANGELOU

When we can see the good in the learners, we open doors and possibilities for them. Valuing the lived experience of each learner in your setting establishes a healthy climate for learning to flourish. Mona Delahooke discusses the power of relationships in her book *Beyond Behaviors* (2019), stressing the importance of establishing a sense of safety through relationships. We can be attuned to our learner's

CHAPTER 3: Building the Zones Climate

physical and emotional needs and tailor our interactions to meet those needs. Through what Delahooke calls "personal attunement" in a relationship, we prioritize a learner's sense of safety and determine what each learner needs, setting the stage for their brains and bodies to be at ease, allowing our learners to be in a responsive state that is calmer and more connected.

Meet the learner where they are, listen to them, and look to understand the causes of their emotions. Support them through their feelings in a way that offers respect, compassion, and safety. To be their partner in their regulation, you must have a relationship. Below are some ways to help build it.

Think About:

- How do I show my learners that I care about and respect them?
- Do I know what is important to them? What are their dreams for themselves?
- What are the strengths of my learners and how can I highlight them?
- How can I establish trust and partnership with my learners and with their families/caregivers?
- Do learners feel supported in expressing a full range of emotions when in my presence?
- What is the frequency of positive reinforcement vs. negative redirections/reminders I communicate?

Actions/Strategies:

- Develop routines and activities that integrate learners' voices, ideas, identities, and values.
- Provide leadership opportunities for learners to showcase their strengths.
- Positively affirm learners, not just for their positive actions, but for their unique identities and contributions to your community—whether that's home, classroom, small group, club, etc.
- Follow through with positive reinforcement; acknowledge and communicate successes, even small ones, with both learners and caregivers.
- Dig into goals and ambitions; sit down with individual learners to find out what goals they have for themselves. These can be short-term, long-term, social goals, or personal goals.

3. CO-REGULATE WITH LEARNERS

As mentioned in Chapter 1, co-regulation is the process of connecting, or being attuned, with a social partner for support in attaining goals, meeting demands, and supporting a sense of well-being. As a Zones leader, you are also a co-regulator. As you teach *The Zones Digital Curriculum*, you concurrently play an important role in co-regulating with your learners. This often comes naturally as we respond, adjust, and flex to our learners throughout the day. For example, every time you take note of where a learner checks in and you acknowledge it in your response, you are co-regulating with them. Co-regulation not only helps build a positive climate and rapport but is essential for helping learners move along in their development of regulation strategies by nourishing more language and metacognitive abilities. The strategies below represent just some of the ways you can co-regulate.

Co-Regulation Strategy	Example
Verbal Cues	"I notice your body is moving fast. Let's do a Zones Check-In."
Non-verbal Cues	Offering a choice board with a toolbox of strategies to select from.
Proximity	Giving a learner more physical space if they are showing Red Zone physiological signals.
Tone of Voice	Maintaining a calm and steady voice when supporting a dysregulated learner.
Adjusting Sensory Demands	Turning down lights, minimizing sounds, adjusting temperature, etc.
Anticipating Triggers	Planning ahead for a trigger, such as a fire drill or difficult transition. Modify or adapt a task that might be triggering.
Proactive Systems and Plans	Build in a proactive sensory or regulation break as part of a learner's routine and Green Zone Toolbox.
Affirmation	"I noticed you set the timer and chose a tool in the Regulation Station. Great job!"
Choice	Offering for a learner to do a Zones Check-In with you, or just check in with themselves privately.
Attunement	Mirroring the emotional state of the other, such as if they are down, using a slower cadence and matching their body language.
Regulating Oneself	Using your own regulation tool when supporting a learner who is dysregulated.

CHAPTER 3: Building the Zones Climate

Think About:

- How do I use non-verbal cues, rather than verbal cues, to communicate with learners?
- How do I adjust the way I'm speaking to a learner when I notice they are dysregulated?
- How often do I offer learners a choice? Could I integrate choice more often?
- What proactive regulation supports are already built into my routine with learners?

Actions/Strategies:

- Increase visual supports for non-verbal communication (such as a Zones Check-In), this benefits all learners (not just those with emergent language).
- Carefully observe a learner's triggers and make proactive plans when you anticipate them happening.
- Build proactive supports into a learner's routine, such as sensory supports or time to connect with trusted adults. Find ways to adjust the sensory input within your setting, including sound, light, temperature, smell, proximity to others, etc.

4. CULTIVATE INCLUSION

At The Zones of Regulation, we believe that it is crucial to support racial equity, neurodiversity, gender diversity, and cultural diversity in schools, clinics, and community-based settings. Most importantly, we see social emotional learning (SEL) as a critical lever for advancing equity and inclusion for all learners and moving away from punitive behavioral models that perpetuate disparities in opportunity and outcomes for marginalized populations such as those who identify as BIPOC or neurodivergent. According to The National Equity Project, "Culturally responsive teaching incorporates and centers unique student experiences and identities, supporting educators to build learning partnerships that result in increased student engagement and ownership of learning," (https://www.nationalequityproject.org/culturally-responsive-teaching). When taught through a culturally responsive, affirming, and value lens, The Zones of Regulation empowers adult leaders to create an emotionally safe and supportive environment

> **"** Inclusion is not bringing people into what already exists; it is making a new space, a better space for everyone."
> —GEORGE J. SEFA DEI, SOCIAL JUSTICE SCHOLAR

that, in turn, sets the stage for all learners to thrive. The critical practice of culturally responsive teaching is underscored by key understandings in cognitive science about the brain's perceptions of safety vs. threat (as discussed in Chapter 1) that impact learning in each environment, as well as how we use culture to make meaning to build skills. Zaretta Hammond, author of *Culturally Responsive Teaching & the Brain* (2015) explains, "Our challenge as culturally responsive teachers is knowing how to create an environment that the brain perceives as safe and nurturing so it can relax, let go of any stress, and turn its attention to learning" (page 50).

One key practice that sets the stage for cultivating inclusion is examining one's biases. These are unconscious or conscious attitudes and stereotypes based on race, gender identity, disability, religion, socioeconomic status, etc., that influence our thoughts and actions. They also impact our perception and treatment of learners, which can be detrimental to their growth in social emotional skills, self-esteem, and academic skills. It is important to know all people have biases and that the work we do to uncover and examine our biases further aligns us with the values we hold to be true.

While we can't totally shed ourselves (or our society at large) of bias, we can take action to cultivate inclusion and belonging in our spaces with intention. This looks like integrating best practices in culturally responsive teaching and further use of neurodiversity- and identity-affirming strategies that respect, reflect, and honor learners' identities and life experiences. The following recommendations are just a starting point on the journey toward more inclusive and equitable climates.

Think About:

- Are biases and ableism present in my setting when discussing and addressing behavioral concerns, compliance, and consequences?

- How do my culture, values, and norms (i.e., voice volume and tone, activity level, body language, eye contact, etc.) factor into my expectations for learners?

- Do I share my own identity with my learners?

- Do I lean in with curiosity to learn about the identity of my learners?

- How does my space honor, value, and reflect all learners' cultures, lived experiences, and identities?

CHAPTER 3: Building the Zones Climate

Actions/Strategies:

- Discuss how all bodies feel differently, and that regulation will look and feel differently for everyone.

- Use imagery and media that is representative of a wide variety of identities, cultures, and life experiences.

- Collaborate with learners on scenarios and examples within instruction that are relevant to their lives.

- Set up systems for group discussion in which learners can explore a variety of perspectives.

- Normalize difference: Highlight how our differences add value to a group or community.

5. MAKE SENSE OF BEHAVIOR

Dr. Ross Greene, an expert psychologist on supporting children with challenging behavior and the creator of Collaborative and Proactive Solutions, reminds us, "Children do well if they can." (*The Explosive Child*, 2005, page 16.) This is a good mantra and mindset for all educators, practitioners, and caregivers working with learners. No child wants the reputation of being "naughty," "the bad kid," or "a behavior problem." Dr. Greene suggests a learner's behavior is communication and may indicate differences in skills, unsolved problems, or simply that something isn't right or working for them. Dr. Greene advocates adults shifting their mindset. He suggests we need to understand that challenging behavior is an experience of how the learner is feeling in the moment, combined with their abilities to manage that feeling. We as adults need to figure out what we can do to support our learners.

> **Kids do well if they can, not if they want to." — DR. ROSS GREENE**

The first step is to be a better observer of our learners. In their book, *The "Why" Behind Classroom Behaviors* (2020), Jamie Chaves and Ashley Taylor explain, "Asking 'why' a student is displaying a certain behavior allows you as a teacher to optimize a learning environment that accommodates all children. As the 'why' is uncovered, better supports and systems can be put in place to address the underlying issue (and help smooth the terrain going forward). Rather than putting a Band-Aid on the behavioral symptoms, we can address the underlying vulnerability." Consider what is "under the hood" and the "terrain" for each learner. Also consider settings and situations, such as time of day, free time vs. structured tasks, and group vs. independent work, that may be affecting regulation.

Let's take a look at a scenario. As an adult, you may feel discomfort when a learner refuses to follow the instruction you gave her to remain seated. Your instinct may be to force her to comply, which likely will lead to a power struggle. However, if you shift your lens to understand that this learner is doing the best she can given the situation, and think through the "why" this may be a challenge for her, you realize she has been seated for a long time. You remember that her sensory system needs to move more than others in the class.

The next step you can take to support your learners' regulation is altering the terrain. Ask yourself, "What obstacles can I remove to make things go smoother for them?" For example, in the situation above, support the learner's terrain by delaying giving any more instruction, and pivot to taking a movement break. Integrating empathy and providing the learner the opportunity to get her sensory needs met allows her to regulate and become ready to take on a new learning challenge. Lastly, by giving her a few choices for how she can demonstrate her learning, you provide her with power and more control.

Keep in mind, all humans work to learn strategies to regulate across our life span, and all of us have shortcomings when it comes to our ability to regulate from time to time—myself included. No one in my family would argue this. I occasionally lose my patience and get irritable when I'm stressed. It's important to offer grace when a learner isn't managing themselves in a situation well, as it's likely they would have rather been able to respond in a different manner. When we embark on using The Zones of Regulation, we need to view the outward behavior of our learners with curiosity and compassion rather than passing judgment. This gives us the opportunity to seek understanding of what a learner's behavior may be communicating.

Think About:

- When do I notice the learner is regulating successfully? What conditions are helping enable them to regulate in this situation?
- What patterns am I seeing in terms of this learner's challenging behavior? (frequency, timing, certain people present)
- Does my setting focus on well-being over compliance with behavioral expectations?
- What might this learner be telling me through their behavior? Is there a perceived threat or a sensory need not being met?
- What's under the hood? Are there underlying skills to develop to support regulating with more ease?

FACTORS IMPACTING REGULATIONS

What's Under the Hood?
Neurobiological Components of Regulation
- Development
- Sensory Processing
- Executive Functioning
- Emotional Regulation
- Social Cognition
- Trauma Exposure/ACEs

What's the Terrain?
External Factors Impacting Regulation
Lived Experience • Culture • Sociopolitical Factors • Access • Relationships

(For more, see Beyond Behavior section, starting on page 6.)

- How has their terrain impacted their regulation abilities? How can I cultivate a terrain that will support the learner's regulation?

Actions/Strategies:

- Spend time with a learner to discover their strengths and interests to build upon.

- Lean in with curiosity and compassion rather than judgment and shame when dysregulation occurs or when behaviors don't meet the demands of the situation.

- Focus on the positive qualities and inherent innocence in each learner.

- Communicate with caregivers and other trusted adults to learn more about the learner's strengths, preferences, and unique qualities.

ESSENTIAL ELEMENTS FOR A ZONES CLIMATE

We have explored how the ways you regulate yourself, build relationships, cultivate inclusion, and make sense of learners' behaviors can profoundly impact the learners' experience. Think of these actions as the foundation on which to build a sound structure. Use these Essential Elements from The Zones of Regulation to help establish the Zones Climate in your setting:

1. Provide direct instruction and practice opportunities.
2. Post Zones Visuals.
3. Offer Zones Check-Ins.
4. Provide easy access to regulation tools.
5. Use Zones language.

THE ZONES CLIMATE CLASSROOM VIGNETTE

Before we go into more detail on each of the Essential Elements of a Zones Climate, let's peek into Mr. Garza's third grade classroom to get an understanding of how a Zones classroom climate can look and feel.

Mr. Garza hears the bustling of lockers opening and closing and morning chatter as third graders pour into the hallway, prompting him to start the calming music in the classroom that the class has agreed helps with their morning transition. As the first group of learners trickles into the classroom, he greets each of them. They, in turn, follow their morning routine to walk over to their Zones Check-In station and move a craft stick with their name on it from a white container into a red, yellow, green, or blue container that corresponds to the Zone they are experiencing. Donte sees Mr. Garza's stick in the Blue Zone and remembers that he's told the class he often feels groggy first thing in the morning. If anyone forgets what each of the Zones represents, they can glance at the visual on the wall that the class created together as a reminder of the four Zones; there are pictures of kids in the class, school staff, and even Minecraft characters (a class favorite) representing feelings in each of the Zones.

As the learners complete their Zones Check-In and make their way to their table groups, Mr. Garza hears Sophia loudly stomp into the room and greets her, "Good morning, Sophia." This is a common transition into the classroom for Sophia, who is often triggered by the noise and chaos of the morning bus ride to school. Sophia stomps right past the Zones Check-In station to her table, leaving her name stick in the white container. Instead of prompting her to check in, Mr. Garza uses this information as a cue that Sophia may need additional time and support this morning. As the learners settle into their morning work, Mr. Garza quietly kneels by Sophia's desk and holds out his lanyard, which has the four Zones colors (blue, green, yellow, red) on a ring as a non-verbal check-in prompt. Sophia swats at the Red Zone, and Mr. Garza says quietly, "You've told me that the mornings can be overwhelming. Would you like to try the Regulation Station? Your choice." Sophia glares at him and puts her head down.

As Mr. Garza circulates the classroom helping with morning work, he sees Sophia stand up and stomp over to the classroom Regulation Station, which is located at the side of the classroom in full sight of the board at the front. Sophia plops down on the cushion on the floor and rustles through the basket of sensory items including a few small fidgets, a pinwheel for deep breaths, and a maze book (tools taught systematically to the whole class) until she finds the noise-cancelling headphones and puts them on. She then flips a sand timer over and looks at a poster beside her that displays the Tool of the Week, a regulation strategy that is introduced every Monday during morning meeting. This week's Zones tool is Reach and Breathe (which is one of the tool cards in the Zones Tools to Try Cards for Kids deck).

CHAPTER 3: Building the Zones Climate

She stretches her arms up into the air and takes a big sighing breath, and then does it again just as the class practiced with Mr. Garza. The 2-minute timer is up, but Sophia remains in the Regulation Station, flipping it one more time and using a fidget item from the basket. Sophia needs more time to regulate her feelings and body, which she and Mr. Garza have agreed upon as a part of her individual plan.

When the sand timer runs out for the second time, Sophia takes her headphones off, places them back in the basket, and walks (without stomping) to the classroom Zones Check-In station and places her name stick in the Yellow Zone container. Mr. Garza connects and says, "Sophia, I love the way I saw you using the Tool of the Week in our Regulation Station. It looks like it helped you feel in more control of your Red Zone. Does that sound right?" Sophia replies, "Yeah, I'm still kinda frustrated in the Yellow though," while looking down at the floor. Mr. Garza gently reminds her, "Remember, all of our Zones are okay. When you get back to your seat, you can check out your Zones Toolbox to see if there might be another tool that would be helpful." As Sophia heads to her desk, Mr. Garza offers, "If you're up for it, would you be willing to demonstrate the Reach and Breath tool during morning meeting?" Sophia hesitantly nods with a small smile in the corner of her mouth.

Mr. Garza heads to the front of the class and dings the chime, prompting the learners to put down their pencils and mindfully listen to the sound. This also signals that it's time to transition to their daily morning meeting. Once seated on the rug, the class does their morning greeting around the circle. Mr. Garza says, "Let's start by looking at our Zones Check-In this morning. What do you notice?" One learner raises their hand and says, "I notice that the Blue Zone has the most sticks in it, including yours Mr. G!" Mr. Garza replies, "I think you're right. It looks like many of our bodies and brains may be moving slowly, and that's okay. Let's take a look at our Zones Poster and think about a tool that can help us regulate our Zones."

Another learner suggests, "What about the Tool of the Week? Can we use Reach and Breath in the Blue Zone?"

Mr. Garza replies, "Yes. We have been learning about different tools that can help us care for our Zones. Let's give it a try and you can notice how it helps you. Sophia, would you like to show us how it's done?"

Getting Into The **Zones** of Regulation

Mr. Garza didn't create this climate overnight. He built it over time, gradually teaching concepts from The Zones of Regulation curriculum, while concurrently integrating the Zones Climate Essential Elements. Let's zoom out to learn more about the specific elements Mr. Garza integrated into his classroom to create this climate.

PROVIDE DIRECT INSTRUCTION AND PRACTICE OPPORTUNITIES
ESSENTIAL ELEMENT 1

"There's not enough time in the day." This is a frequent complaint we hear from many leaders. We understand and empathize with the pressures you are under to find the time to teach The Zones along with all your other responsibilities. But scheduling and protecting instructional time to directly teach skills from The Zones of Regulation curriculum (rather than just hanging up a visual) is critical to learners' growth and progress in social emotional learning. Research into school-based SEL bears out that access to high-quality social emotional learning instruction is well worth the time invested and is evidenced by positive academic, mental health, and future outcomes for learners. In addition to setting aside time for direct instruction, continuing to touch on concepts throughout the day and week helps learners to practice, generalize, and deepen their understanding. Although The Zones provides flexibility in how it can be implemented across settings and learner populations, there are best practices for when and how to implement and provide direct instruction, modeling, and practice.

For information on implementing *The Zones of Regulation Digital Curriculum,* see Chapter 4.

POST ZONES VISUALS
ESSENTIAL ELEMENT 2

(Following instruction in Concept 2)

The Zones of Regulation graphics and visual supports included in *The Zones of Regulation Digital Curriculum* are carefully thought-out to facilitate understanding, communication, and accessibility for learners and the adults who support them. As you work your way through the curriculum, post and reference related visuals such as Feelings in Each Zone (see figure), Zones Check-In, Zones

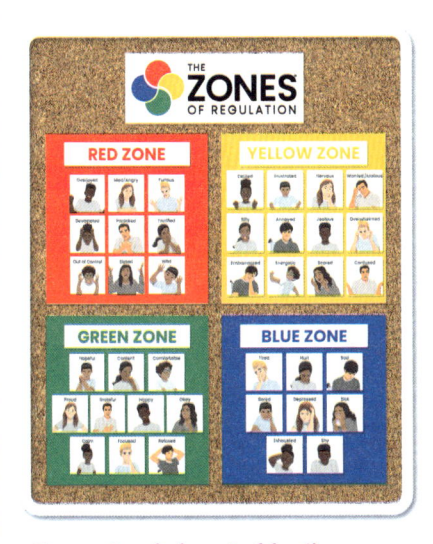

Example of visual of feelings in each Zone, *The Zones of Regulation Digital Curriculum* (2024).

Toolbox, and the Zones Pathway. These visuals will help learners practice and generalize the concepts taught across settings in the following ways. (In addition, there are six Zones posters available individually or as a set from www.socialthinking.com.)

- Provide accessibility for a wide range of learners, including language learners and learners with limited/emergent communication or divergence in auditory processing. For example, rather than a learner trying to decode and decipher what the adult is saying, a visual support can be referenced to give more context to or replace the receptive language (what is being communicated to the learner). This same visual can also help the learner with their expressive language (or communication) of how they feel or what they need.

- Provide a non-verbal communication strategy for both learners and supporting adults, creating a visual communication system. For example, when a learner changes Zones in the middle of a lesson and can share this with classroom staff by moving an indicator on their Zones Check-In. This prompts staff to connect with the learner for support.

- Increase the likelihood that regulation skills will be recalled and used in the moment.

- Show that you value well-being, and that regulating The Zones is welcome in that environment.

While many of the key visuals in *The Zones of Regulation® Digital Curriculum* have multiple versions for easy differentiation, it is important to adapt them to be relevant to, representative of, and engaging for your learning population. Be sure to use a critical eye for bias when exploring imagery/media to incorporate into visuals. A best practice is to create Zones Visuals along with learners, allowing for discussions as you negotiate topics such as how some emotions may fit into more than one Zone, what emotions should be displayed for each Zone, etc. Post visuals in common areas where learners spend time, and at their eye-height to increase accessibility.

Considerations for Zones Visuals

- **Age/developmental stage**: Use imagery of people who are representative of your learners. For example, when working with teen or adult learners use imagery of similar-age learners when representing emotions and situations.

- **Language:** Use vocabulary that is accessible for learners, including providing translated or multi-lingual visuals for those who may benefit. For example, limit emotional vocabulary to just 1–3 emotions per Zone for learners with emergent emotional vocabulary and understanding.

- **Accessibility:** Integrate assistive technology, familiar visual imagery, and best practices for learners with additional access needs/barriers. For example, create your Zones Visual using a common adaptive visual system such as Boardmaker, and add The Zones into communication boards and devices.

- **Cultural relevance:** Use imagery, iconography, and media that is culturally relevant and representative of your learners. For example, consider using photos of learners and familiar adults in Zones Visuals.

- **Interest areas:** Incorporate interest areas into visuals for engagement. For example, create a Zones Visual with favorite characters, athletes, or musicians showcasing the various emotions within each Zone.

Source: Image from *Tools to Try for Tweens & Teens* deck by Leah Kuypers and Elizabeth Sautter (Social Thinking, 2020).

CHAPTER 3: Building the Zones Climate

OFFER ZONES CHECK-INS
ESSENTIAL ELEMENT 3
(Following instruction from Concept 5: The Zones Check-In)

As we learned in Chapter 2, the Zones Check-In is a mindful awareness practice when we pause to tune in to our body's signals, emotions, and Zones. Embedding the Signature Practice of Zones Check-Ins into your environment and daily routines promotes the development of emotional vocabulary, self-awareness, and regulation. Learners, as well as leaders, might do a Zones Check-In within a structured system, such as using a check-in visual included with *The Zones Digital Curriculum* (see the *Zones Check-In Visual*, left) or moving an object (like their name card, photo, or craft stick) to something that represents each Zone, as Sophia from Mr. Garza's class did in the vignette in the beginning of this chapter. Once learners become more familiar, check-ins may become more informal and less structured. Learners may just check in with themselves as a self-monitoring and mindfulness strategy. Adolescents might seek more discreet ways to check in and communicate their Zone, such as using American Sign Language (ASL) to sign the color of their Zone or a corresponding-colored highlighter on their desk. We recommend adapting your Zones Check-In to meet the needs of your learners (using the same considerations listed in the Post Zones Visuals section).

As adult co-regulators, a Zones Check-In gives you an opportunity to connect with your learners and be attuned to their needs. For example, if you notice a learner is routinely checking in within the Blue Zone at the beginning of a group session, you can introduce activities that help re-energize them to prepare for learning. You can also use a Zones Check-In as your first line of support, rather than starting with a behavior correction or redirection. This "feelings first" approach can have a positive impact on relationships and the climate of a home, classroom, or other setting. Be mindful not to publicly over-focus on moments when one learner is in a Zone that differs from those around them. There should never be any shame associated with how we feel or our Zones.

No matter how your check-in looks, it is critically important that a Zones Check-In system is not tied to a punitive or disciplinary response. This means we're not rewarding learners for being in the Green Zone, or having consequences tied to being in the Blue, Yellow, or Red Zones. Learners need to feel comfortable using The Zones to express their feelings and know that all Zones are okay. Consider using a Zones Check-In system in place of a behavior or classroom management system.

CONSIDERATION FOR ZONES CHECK-INS

DOs

- ✓ **DO** model first by Owning Your Zone and checking in with all of your Zones to establish a safe climate that values all feelings.

- ✓ **DO** use a Zones Check-In as a non-judgmental communication strategy, reinforcing that ALL ZONES ARE OKAY.

- ✓ **DO** consider that checking in can feel hard for some learners due to self-awareness and their sense of safety and comfort in the situation.

- ✓ **DO** use observations and inquiry when checking in with learners. For example, "I see that your head is down, and you are yawning. What Zone are you in?"

- ✓ **DO** check-ins throughout the day to allow for self-reflection in all Zones.

DON'Ts

- ✗ **DON'T** make checking in one-sided just for learners. We all experience all of The Zones.

- ✗ **DON'T** connect a Zones Check-In to a compliance or punitive system. Remember: The Zones is not a behavior management system; there should be no rewards or punishments for being in any Zone.

- ✗ **DON'T** force someone to check in. It is crucial to respect the autonomy of each unique individual.

- ✗ **DON'T** label somebody's Zone for them. This can lead to misunderstanding and misinterpretation.

- ✗ **DON'T** only use Zones Check-Ins during challenging moments.

For more information on the Zones Check-In, see Chapter 2. In addition, Concept 5 in *The Zones Digital Curriculum* is devoted to the Zones Check-In.

EASY ACCESS TO REGULATION TOOLS
ESSENTIAL ELEMENT 4
(Following instruction of Concept 7)

A Zones Climate welcomes the use of tools as the norm, not the exception. It's important that you help learners see and understand that regulation "tools" and strategies are all around us: the water we drink to keep us feeling well, getting up to move to keep us focused, connecting with a friend to blow off some steam, etc. When we consider all the tools or strategies we use to help us regulate, our Zones Toolbox may be overflowing.

CHAPTER 3: Building the Zones Climate

Top: Image from page 43, *The Regulation Station* storybook, by Leah Kuypers and Elizabeth Sautter (Social Thinking, 2021)

Bottom: "Comfort Spot" card from the *Tools to Try for Kids* deck by Leah Kuypers and Elizabeth Sautter (Social Thinking, 2020)

Emphasize that each of us needs different tools to help us regulate and that our toolbox is unique to us. Some learners may require regulation tools that others don't need, and that is fair. Fair doesn't mean equal, rather equity is everyone getting what they need; for some learners, that may be access to specialized tools such a swing in the school's sensory room or a T-stool to adapt the seating. When you take time to build the Zones Climate, you create an inclusive setting where everyone accessing the regulation tools they need is expected.

To support a Zones Climate in a community setting such as a school, it is recommended that learners have access to regulation tools in places where they spend time, including in general education classrooms, specialist rooms (art, music, physical education, etc.), health and front offices, and common spaces such as the cafeteria, hallways, and playground. Having tools or visuals of Zones Toolboxes that include a menu of options (most tools do not involve a physical object being present) in multiple places allows learners to access regulation support without having to leave their peer environment to find it. They can remain in community.

We have found one of the most valuable tools taught with The Zones is a Regulation Station. This is a safe, non-punitive space designated for learners to access for regulation purposes. This can go by many names: "sensory space," "comfort corner," "break area," to name a few. These spaces can be set up in homes, classrooms, community, and therapeutic settings to help both leaders and learners regulate. These spaces should feel comfortable and can grow to house a variety of tools for each Zone. In addition to including a Regulation Station in classrooms, many schools have another designated space within the building such as a sensory room, Zen Den, or Zones room, for learners who need additional support, sensory tools, or more privacy.

There are several factors to think through when introducing a Regulation Station to learners, particularly within a larger group setting. While many of these best practices are geared toward classrooms, they can easily be adapted for the home and/or therapeutic spaces.

Considerations for Tools and Regulation Stations

- Set aside time to reflect as a community on which tools seem to be most effective, and whether some tools need guidelines for use.

- Model using tools yourself. You can say, "I'm in the _____ Zone. I am going to use ____ tool to help me take care of my Zone."

- Don't emphasize that learners need to use tools to "get back to the Green Zone." This may be harmful to some learners, because it doesn't honor their unique state. Instead, you can say, "We use our tools to help us care for our Zone and work toward our goals."

- A Regulation Station is a non-punitive space and should not be seen as a negative by learners. It is NOT a place to send a learner when "in trouble," rather a neutral place to be to help them manage their Zones.

- Consider naming the Regulation Station together as a group to engage learners and promote ownership of their community space.

- The Regulation Station can be a tool for ANY of the Zones. Some learners who are quick to go to the Red Zone may benefit from proactively using the Regulation Station as a Green Zone tool to support them maintaining a sense of well-being by giving their nervous systems a chance to relax.

- Spend time systematically teaching and practicing use of the space as a tool, as well as how to use each additional tool that might be housed in the Regulation Station before offering it.

- Expect all learners to be curious when you first introduce the Regulation Station, so give them time to explore it. Set aside time for each learner to visit before officially opening it up for use (for example, learners whose name starts with A–M can give it a try before lunch, those with N–Z after lunch).

- Establish expectations around how to use the Regulation Station, such as how many learners, how often, appropriate use, clean-up, and respect for materials in it. Some learners may need to use it more frequently than others and this can be framed in a conversation around equity vs. equality.

- Placement suggestions (in a traditional classroom): Set up an area, preferably off to the side of the room but not in back. Ideally, learners can still see and hear instruction but not have to be right in the mix of all the sensory stimuli. There is a balance between privacy and safety/inclusion.

- As a group, establish a reasonable time for how long to use the Regulation Station (consider a timer or visual), and practice transitioning out of this space. Remind learners, "Tools help us regulate and do our jobs as learners, but they don't replace the work we need to do." If time is up and a learner needs more

CHAPTER 3: Building the Zones Climate

support regulating, gently encourage them to pick a different tool or reset the timer.

- Some learners need the lower sensory load that this space provides. Avoid having problem-solving conversations here. This area is primarily used to support their regulation needs; those conversations can happen after they are in a more regulated state outside of this area.

USE ZONES LANGUAGE
ESSENTIAL ELEMENT 5

Using Zones language creates a positive climate that values a person's feelings over their behavior, and also helps reinforce and apply concepts being taught, such as All The Zones Are Okay and Let's Check In with Our Zones! It is important that all supportive adults embed Zones language and vocabulary across settings to support inclusion, consistency, and co-regulation. The words you use to interact with, prompt, and redirect learners are invaluable teaching tools. For example, replacing common directives such as, "You need to calm down," with language that cultivates competency, "Let's go check in with The Zones," helps learners build skills in self-awareness and co-regulation. This gentle co-regulation provides learners agency to name (and potentially regulate) their feeling and Zone while deepening their self-awareness. Intentionally using the plural *let's* signals to the learner that you are an invested partner with them, checking in alongside them. With learner permission, you can help by stating observations of them to support them in the regulation process. For example, if a learner is unable to identify how they are feeling, you may ask, "Would you like me to help you and share what I am noticing?" If granted, you might say, "I see your head is down and bottom lip is out. Maybe you are feeling sad in the Blue Zone?" (This works best when you can also reference a visual of The Zones and point to the sad feeling.) You can follow this up with tool options to support regulation. "Maybe a tool will help, let's take a look at our Blue Zone Toolbox." You will find that over time, you build a "muscle memory" for skill-based language, and that it's contagious with your learners and other adults in your setting—naturally building a common language within and between learning environments.

> The words you use to interact with, prompt, and redirect learners are invaluable teaching tools. For example, replacing common directives such as, "You need to calm down," with language that cultivates competency, "Let's go check in with The Zones," helps learners build skills in self-awareness and co-regulation.

Own Your Zone

Use of Zones language is not just for your learners. You, and other leaders, can model using Zones language by "owning your zone" (when appropriate). This might mean sharing when triggers or sparks move you between Zones, or sharing how you managed your Zone in a healthy way—or maybe didn't and how that impacted your goals. For example, share a time you were really worried in the Yellow Zone about something, making it challenging for you to focus on your work. Or a time you were in the Red Zone, feeling elated, as you watched your favorite football team win a big game, as well as when you felt angry in the Red Zone because there was a big problem you encountered. Owning your zone in real time is saying things like, "I'm feeling really tired in the Blue Zone, and it's hard for me to think straight." Modeling your Zones not only helps validate the various feelings learners also experience, but also invites them to co-regulate (such as a learner saying, "Miss Leah, you should get a cup of coffee...") and helps build rapport. By being transparent about your own Zones, feelings, triggers, and tools, you are sharing your metacognitive thought process, letting them see into the inner workings of regulation and acknowledging the effort it takes for you to regulate. It also demystifies the regulation process and sets a tone of emotional safety. As you own your zone, consider healthy boundaries between adults and learners, making sure to only share what is appropriate and not "unloading" on your learners or creating a situation where you are depending on them to co-regulate you.

Considerations for Zones Language

- Find opportunities to acknowledge when a learner is regulated within a specific Zone—versus only when dysregulated in a Zone—such as, "It is so fun being silly with you in the Yellow Zone," or, "Nice job using your tools to care for your Yellow Zone."

- Point out when learners may be in the Blue, Yellow, or Red Zone in positive or neutral ways such as, "Wow, I saw you kick that home run! Was that a Red Zone feeling you were having?" or, "I bet many of you are exhausted in the Blue Zone after the mile run in PE."

- Avoid learners only hearing about The Zones when they are experiencing uncomfortable emotions or the mismanagement of them. Having this association may lead them to shut down when The Zones are mentioned.

CHAPTER 3: Building the Zones Climate

ZONES LANGUAGE TO USE WITH LEARNERS

INSTEAD OF...	TRY...
"You need to calm down."	"Let's do a Zones Check-In."
"It's too loud in here."	"The noise in here is making ME feel like I'm in the Yellow Zone, and it's hard for me to think. I need to take a deep breath to manage my Zone."
"You need to take a break."	"How are you feeling? Should we try a tool?"
"You are losing points/getting clipped up on our level system."	"Let's check in with The Zones." If unable to identify a feeling or Zone, with permission, you might go on to say, "It looks like your body has a lot of energy and you are having a hard time focusing. Maybe you are feeling silly in the Yellow Zone. What's a tool that might help?"
"Don't worry about that."	"How can I help with this feeling?"
"You need to get back to the Green Zone."	"It is okay to be angry in the Red Zone and have a safe body. Let's find a tool to help." (And show a visual of their Red Zone Toolbox choices.)

- As learners begin to use the Zones language, recognize their achievements. For example, if a learner communicates that she is in the Red Zone when she is mad, rather than running out of the room (as has been the norm), once she is calm let her know that you are proud that she told you about her Zone.

Above are examples of Zones language to use with learners.

RESPONDING TO BEHAVIOR IN THE MOMENT

As stated in Chapter 2, The Zones of Regulation is not a compliance or behavior management system. As learners explore the concepts within The Zones curriculum, expect that there will be times when they struggle to regulate given the circumstances around them and their capacity in the moment. During those instances, look for triggers that may be contributing to the dysregulation and offer support as a co-regulator. Invite the learner to share their insights through a collaborative approach. If you have established a relationship, learners will be much more receptive to your co-regulation attempts.

As an adult leader, you will need to make a judgment call of when learners are in a state where you can present an option to check in with The Zones and support them in using regulation tools and strategies. Find success with learners checking in in the Blue, Green, and Yellow Zones before offering check-ins when they are in the Red Zone. There are times when learners will be dysregulated beyond the point of even mentioning The Zones and we highly recommend orienting yourself to de-escalation practices, such as Nonviolent Crisis Intervention® (Crisis Prevention Institute; CPI Training; www.crisisprevention.com) to guide you in supporting learners when they are dysregulated and exhibiting unsafe behaviors.

Consider a learner's regulation skills and access to supports/instruction when considering consequences and/or restorative practices. Remember, when thinking about how to manage a consequence, be thinking about what experience the learner needs in order to grow their skills to better navigate future similar situations. Any consequences should not be associated with their Zone, but rather in connection to their behavior, and it is best if a consequence is as natural as possible. For example, if a learner is upset in the Red Zone and tore down the class artwork, later they may need to clean up the mess and repair with peers. This is not because they were in the Red Zone, rather because their actions of destroying others' work and space was hurtful and scary. Restorative practices can help guide those repair conversations.

RESTORATIVE PRACTICES

Restorative practices—also called positive discipline and/or restorative justice—are a powerful approach rooted in interconnectedness at the community level. They are based on knowledge and traditions from Indigenous communities and communities of color worldwide, and nurture a sense of shared humanity rather than compliance and expectations. The Zones of Regulation common language and strategies can be integrated into Restorative Practices to elevate learners' voice, agency, and social connectedness both proactively and reactively. This can look like using The Zones to identify feelings in a restorative circle, working through the impact one's dysregulated behavior has had on others, and/or making proactive plans for how to build a truly inclusive setting.

CHAPTER 3: Building the Zones Climate

The Zones of Regulation Pathway

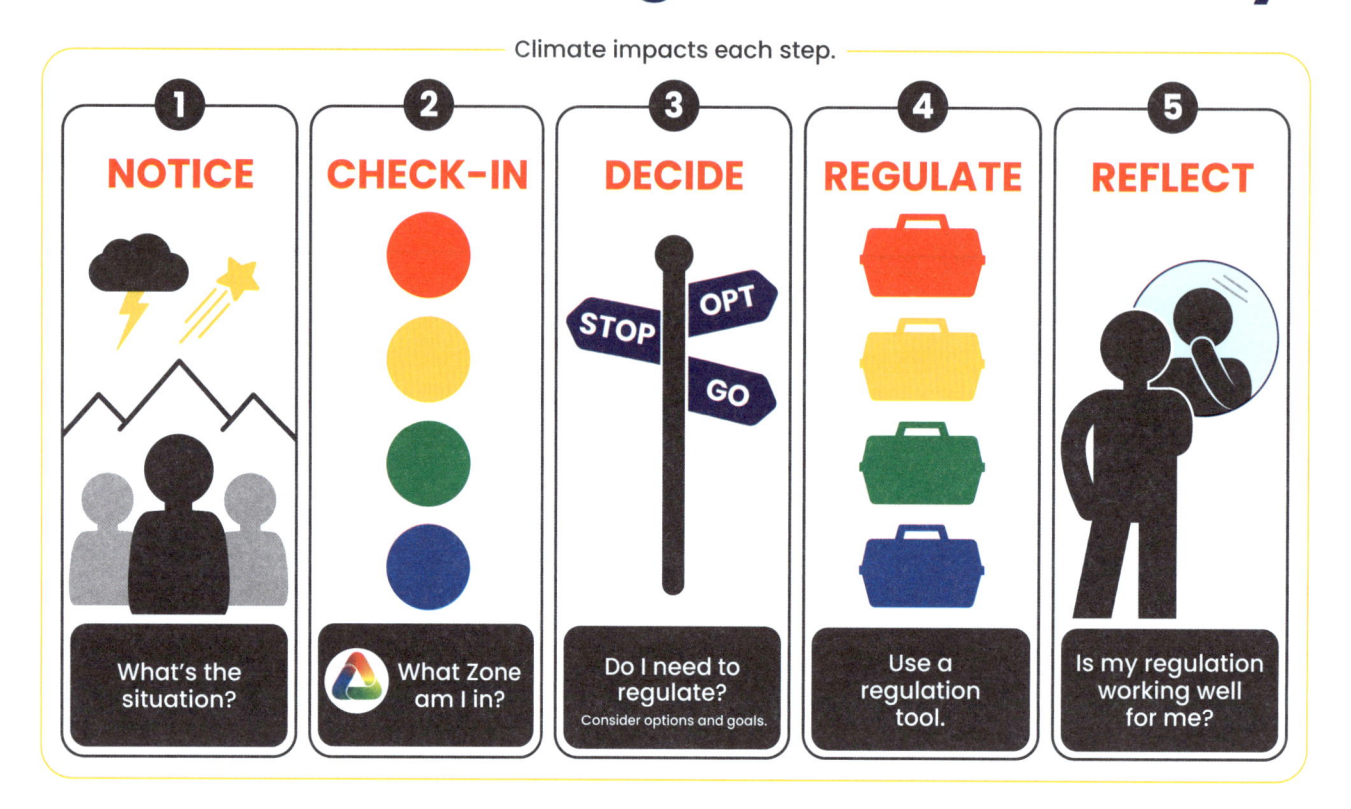

Climate impacts each step.

1. NOTICE — What's the situation?

2. CHECK-IN — What Zone am I in?

3. DECIDE — Do I need to regulate? Consider options and goals.

4. REGULATE — Use a regulation tool.

5. REFLECT — Is my regulation working well for me?

CONTEXT AND CLIMATE IMPACTING THE ZONES PATHWAY

As we've explored throughout this chapter, context (the situation) and climate both significantly impact our access and capacity to regulate. With that in mind, let's reexamine the same scenario that we walked through when discussing the Zones Pathway in Chapter 2, this time noticing how both context and climate factor into feelings, reactions, and regulation. Keep in mind, as we've established, that someone who feels safe and supported in a climate where The Zones is the norm is going to be able to regulate with more ease than someone who does not.

As we can see when we revisit this example, the supportive Zones Climate and culture within the school had a positive impact on regulation. The foundational climate that we build paves the way for our learners (and ourselves) to have a smoother journey.

CLIMATE AND CONTEXT IMPACT ON NAVIGATING THE ZONES PATHWAY

1

NOTICE: What's the situation?

Using your senses, you take in the situation. You consider your surroundings and recognize your trigger. It can sometimes be challenging to pause and notice the situation if you have less comfort and/or trust established there.

EXAMPLE: You are a middle-school-age learner in the hallway between classes, surrounded by many peers and teachers (situation). On the bulletin board, you see a posting of who got a part in the school play. You see the bad news on the bulletin board that you didn't get a part—but you are surrounded by teachers who know you. There is mutual respect between you and the teachers, and school rules are clear: no swearing in the halls, no leaving the building without a pass.

2

CHECK-IN: What Zone am I in?

Understanding the situation/context in which we experience an emotion can help us make sense of it and label it more effectively. In addition, feeling comfortable in a climate allows you to express your feeling/Zone free from judgment or shame.

EXAMPLE: You fully expected to get a part in the play. Learning you didn't make the cast, you feel overwhelmed with anger, mostly at yourself for not practicing more before the try-outs. Rather than suppress your feelings, you acknowledge your Red Zone. You also recognize you will miss hanging out with your theater friends.

3

DECIDE: Do I need to regulate?

In figuring out how to regulate, context continues to factor in as you consider your options. You also factor in the people in your setting regarding your social goals, and your experiences of regulating in that setting.

EXAMPLE: In determining how to respond to your Red Zone feelings, you know your school values well-being and encourages using healthy regulation tools. You have the urge to curse out loud or slam your fist into a locker. However, you recognize that if you display this reaction right in front of the teacher, it may interfere with your goal of staying out of trouble and it may frighten your peers.

4

REGULATE: Use a regulation tool.

Context impacts how, when, or where you use your tools, potentially making use more discreet. Climate affects if you feel safe engaging with your tools without judgment and feel supported while using them.

EXAMPLE: You decide to head to the bathroom where it is quieter and more private to do your deep breathing and gain composure. You know if you're a couple minutes late to class, your teacher will understand when you explain the situation and how you needed to use some tools in the moment to regulate.

5

REFLECT: Is my regulation working well for me?

Awareness of your situation integrates with your critical thinking and reflection as you move on with your day or feel comfortable to revisit the pathway.

EXAMPLE: Your teacher checks in with you when you enter and you feel comfortable sharing with them. You congratulate a friend who makes the play and share with them that you are really bummed you didn't get a part. Your friend co-regulates with you, letting you know they are also really bummed you didn't get a part.

CHAPTER 3: Building the Zones Climate

Zones Climate Rubric

Digital Curriculum Implementation and Fidelity Checklist

ZONES CLIMATE ASSESSMENT TOOLS

These resources help Zones leaders assess their implementation and monitor their progress toward building a Zones Climate in their setting.

The Zones Climate Rubric (Appendix, page 133) can be used to build understanding, reflect, monitor, and set goals for each of the Essential Elements of the Zones Climate.

Digital Curriculum Implementation & Fidelity Checklist (Appendix, page 148) is used to score implementation fidelity on key elements of the curriculum, including climate.

Neither tool is meant to pass judgment on Zones leaders, but rather to set goals and monitor progress toward creating a climate of well-being, which is a process that happens over time.

CONCLUSION

A supportive climate where there is trust and rapport between learners and facilitators is not only a trauma-informed practice, but is also a best practice (and essential) for The Zones of Regulation implementation and thereby allows learners to flourish. Given that The Zones represents our feelings, the climate in which it is taught is critically important—it is essential to create a safe and inclusive space that fosters connection and well-being. This sets the stage for learners to feel comfortable as they learn to identify and communicate (or not, if they choose) their feelings and Zones, as well as practice and use their regulation tools (if and when they are ready). This work begins with the adult leader's mindset and the relationships they build with learners, as well as the Essential Elements of The Zones that are integrated within a learning environment. Please know that building a Zones Climate does not happen overnight. This is a process that takes time and care as both leaders and learners gain comfort with The Zones of Regulation.

APPLY YOUR LEARNING

Use the following activities to process what you learned in this chapter about actions you can take to cultivate a Zones Climate.

Reflection Questions

1. In the Essential Elements of a Zones Climate, you learned strategies for building a climate that fosters well-being. Re-read the Classroom Climate Vignette on page (68) and complete the Leader Reflection Activity: Identifying the Zones Climate Practices sheet.

2. Use the Leader Reflection Activity: Building the Foundation for Regulation: My Actions to set goals for building a Zones Climate in your setting. Think about the practices you can integrate as you begin implementing The Zones, and which ones you will build in later as you work through the curriculum concepts.

3. What are your next steps?

Pair & Share with a Colleague

- Think about the climates you navigated growing up, including classrooms, teams or clubs, organizations, religious institutions, social groups, etc. Describe a climate in which you felt a sense of well-being. What were the characteristics? Was there a climate where you felt discomfort? What were the characteristics?

- Refer to the examples within "Essential Element 5: Use Zones Language" on page 78. What are some other common phrases you often use in your setting? What can you say instead, incorporating Zones language?

- Discuss how the example in The Zones of Regulation Pathway on page 83 might change if the context was different. For example:

    a. If the learner was new to the school and didn't know anyone

    b. If the learner's school has strict consequences for many behavioral "infractions"

    c. If the learner was a racial or cultural minority within the school

    d. If the learner has a history of self-injurious behavior

    e. If the learner has negative relationships with school staff/teachers

LEADER REFLECTION ACTIVITY: CHAPTER 3

BUILDING THE FOUNDATION FOR REGULATION: MY ACTIONS

DIRECTIONS: Reflect on the Think About and Actions/Strategies recommended in *Building the Foundation for Regulation* (pages 59–68). Identify your priorities and complete the boxes below for each practice.

	Notice or think about:	Action or strategy to try:
1. REGULATE YOURSELF		
2. BUILD RELATIONSHIPS		
3. CO-REGULATE WITH LEARNERS		
4. CULTIVATE INCLUSION		
5. MAKE SENSE OF BEHAVIOR		

LEADER REFLECTION ACTIVITY: CHAPTER 3

IDENTIFYING THE ZONES CLIMATE PRACTICES

DIRECTIONS: Re-read the The Zones Climate Classroom Vignette on page 68. Identify and list examples of how the classroom teacher integrated each of the Essential Elements of the Zones Climate into their setting.

1. Provide direct instruction and practice opportunities.

_____

2. Post Zones Visuals.

_____

3. Offer Zones Check-Ins.

_____

4. Make regulation tools accessible.

_____

5. Use Zones language.

Reflect: Mark examples you would like to try in your setting.

CHAPTER 4
TEACHING THE ZONES OF REGULATION CURRICULUM

OVERVIEW AND GOALS

The first three chapters of this book have been about shifting your lens to best support regulation development in your learners, priming you with the background information on The Zones of Regulation and the Signature Practices that constitute "doing The Zones," and providing suggestions to facilitate a Zones Climate. In this chapter, you will learn all you need to know about *The Zones of Regulation® Digital Curriculum* (sold separately via subscription at www.zonesofregulaton.com), including the following:

- An overview of *The Zones of Regulation Digital Curriculum*; how it's organized, the concepts and skills it covers, and the components included.

- How to implement *The Zones Digital Curriculum,* including instructional tips and resources on pacing, differentiation, communication with families and team members, and measuring progress.

- Where to implement *The Zones Digital Curriculum* and how to support use in homes, clinical settings, classrooms, and after-school/community centers.

As I shared in the Preface, The Zones of Regulation has evolved since it was first published in 2011. I recognized that a digital curriculum would best meet the needs of the various types of leaders, as well as the learners. Given the prominent use of visuals throughout The Zones, a digital format not only made instruction delivery easier for

> **GOAL FOR CHAPTER**
>
> - Gain the knowledge and confidence you need to implement *The Zones of Regulation Digital Curriculum* with your learners.

CHAPTER 4: Teaching The Zones of Regulation Digital Curriculum

> **Zones Connection: Individualized Progress**
>
> The focus of The Zones of Regulation is for all learners to build competencies in regulation within their own developmental continuum and make progress on their authentic goals.

leaders, but also more engaging and accessible for learners. The information in this chapter speaks to the new *The Zones of Regulation® Digital Curriculum*, and some of this information also applies to the original book, *The Zones of Regulation*™.

INTRODUCTION TO *THE ZONES OF REGULATION® DIGITAL CURRICULUM*

The Zones of Regulation Digital Curriculum has many new features, while also incorporating the best of the original curriculum. These key features include:

- Easy-to-teach with ready-to-use interactive presentations, activities, and videos with step-by-step guidance to support successful implementation by leaders with a range of backgrounds and regulation experiences.

- Accessible via an online platform (website) that includes a mix of digital and non-digital activities for learners, a variety of engaging interactive mediums, and valuable incorporation of visual learning assets.

- Flexible implementation models that easily apply to small groups, whole classrooms, or one-on-one instruction in a range of settings including school, home, therapy, and community-based programs.

- Integration of principles from Universal Design for Learning (UDL), to facilitate **all** learners from school-age (around 5 years of age) through adults being able to access and apply the content. Each concept offers differentiated activities to meet the needs of learners across the age and developmental spectrum.

- Ten concepts, which are expanded versions of a traditional lesson, designed to be taught across multiple sessions.

- Tool of the Week menu to structure, explore, and reflect on a variety of regulation tools and strategies.

SCOPE AND SEQUENCE

The concepts within the curriculum build upon each other, with later concepts expanding upon skills, lessons, and vocabulary taught in earlier concepts. For example, learners need to name and explain the four Zones of Regulation (Concept 2) before they can check in in each of the four Zones (Concept 5).

> **Age Guidance**
>
> *The Zones of Regulation Digital Curriculum* includes numerous resources that extend and adapt learning to ages 4 through adult, however, the Interactive Presentations were developed for learners 8 and above. Language will need to be modified for use with younger learners and those with emergent language. The comprehensive Concept Guides have many suggestions for scaffolded learning to help you make teaching meaningful and engaging for a wide spectrum of learners.

- **Concepts 1–6: Foster self-, social, and situational awareness.** After defining regulation, the focus is on building emotional awareness by first exploring feelings and states in others and how they relate to The Zones, establishing that all our feelings and Zones are okay. Then we advance to self-exploration, including identifying interoceptive body sensations and signals that help learners recognize how they are feeling. Learning progresses to the Zones Check-In, teaching learners to be mindful in the moment of how they are feeling. Learning culminates with learners digging into situational awareness and its impact on their feelings/Zones. This includes exploring the triggers and sparks that affect their feelings and regulation. Understanding different perspectives is woven across concepts.

- **Concepts 7–10: Explore and apply regulation and decision-making strategies.** We begin the second half of the curriculum by introducing regulation tools and how they help to regulate each Zone. Learners explore various tools and strategies with the Tool of the Week and create a customized Zones Toolbox. Next, the focus shifts to supporting learners in decision-making around regulation, including using Stop, Opt & Go as a strategy to pause before we act, think through our options, and use our goals to help decide what option will work well. Learning culminates with The Zones of Regulation Pathway, which provides concrete steps to apply the concepts taught in real time, while deepening learners' metacognitive regulation strategies and self-reflection abilities.

(See The Zones of Regulation Digital Curriculum Map, page 92, to be taught over the course of time, with learning targets for each concept.)

**The Zones of Regulation Digital Curriculum* will continue to expand with new concepts and resources offered over time. Please refer to the scope and sequence within *The Zones Digital Curriculum* for the most up-to-date curriculum map and materials.

CONCEPT COMPONENTS

Although *The Zones of Regulation Digital Curriculum* is accessed through a subscription-based online digital platform, the instructional resources themselves are a mix of digital and non-digital supports. Each concept includes the following parts:

CONCEPT GUIDE: Provides leaders with detailed step-by-step instruction for teaching each concept, much like what one would

Continued on page 93

Zones Connection:

If you haven't yet subscribed to *The Zones of Regulation® Digital Curriculum,* follow the instructions provided in the back of the book to gain your free, six-month access to Concept 1.

CHAPTER 4: Teaching The Zones of Regulation Digital Curriculum

THE ZONES OF REGULATION DIGITAL CURRICULUM MAP

These concepts foster self-, social, and situational awareness.

Concept 1   Concept 2   Concept 3   Concept 4   Concept 5   Concept 6

These concepts explore and apply regulation and decision-making strategies.

Concept 7   Concept 8   Concept 9   Concept 10

Concept Learning Targets

C1 What Is Regulation?
- I can use the word "regulate" in a sentence.
- I can describe one or more ways a person may regulate themselves.

C2 Introducing The Zones of Regulation
- I can name and describe the four Zones of Regulation.
- I can sort, or categorize, feelings into the four Zones of Regulation.

C3 All The Zones Are Okay
- I can connect my feelings and Zones with real-life situations.
- I can give an example of how people have different feelings and perspectives in a situation.

C4 My Signals, My Zones
- I can name at least one body signal I feel when I am in each Zone.
- I can explain how body signals, Zones, and emotions are all connected.

C5 The Zones Check-In
- I can pause and do a Zones Check-In on my own or with others.
- With practice, I can check in when I am in each of the Zones: Red, Yellow, Green, Blue.

C6 Situations that Trigger and Spark
- I can notice and describe the situation around me (when, where, what, who).
- I can name two of my triggers and two of my sparks.

C7 What Is a Regulation Tool?
- I can identify common regulation tools around me.
- I can use The Zones of Regulation to categorize regulation tools.

C8 Building My Zones Toolbox
- I can reflect on how a tool helps me regulate.
- I can share a helpful tool from each Zone in my toolbox.

C9 Deciding to Regulate
- I can pause to think about my options and goals before acting.
- I can decide if using a regulation tool will help in a situation.

C10 The Zones Pathway
- I can use the Zones Pathway in real-time situations.
- Using the Zones Pathway, I can reflect on how my regulation is working for me.

Continued from page 91

see in a lesson plan. In addition to instructional and planning guidance, key parts include:

- What and Why section offering essential background information for Zones leaders to build comfort and understanding around skills being taught
- Trauma-informed and Culturally Responsive practices
- Teaching Tips for scaffolding, deepening, and extending
- Accessibility and Adaptations for more support
- Alternative Activities to supplement or replace select digital activities with real objects or "live" off-screen instruction
- Extend Learning, which includes Zones Climate ideas for integrating and extending key lesson concepts into the learner's environment, as well as the More Zones Resources that include recommendations for optional ancillary Zones products that support, reinforce, or extend the concept being taught.

INTERACTIVE PRESENTATION: Learner-facing slides, activities, and videos designed to engage learners through instruction via Smartboard, screen, projector, computer, or tablet. Each concept's Interactive Presentation includes the following components.

LEARNING TARGETS: Learner-facing objectives

KEY VOCABULARY: Essential terminology

HOOK: A brief activity that engages learners and "hooks" them on the lesson

CORE LESSON: Direct instruction on learning targets

GROUP ACTIVITY: A hands-on activity that helps learners meaningfully apply the Learning Targets

GEARED ACTIVITIES: A menu of supplemental differentiated activities designed to apply, extend, or reinforce concepts being taught. These enrichment activities support learners across a developmental continuum of abilities.

WRAP UP: Learners review the Learning Targets and key concept information, while also being prompted to consider ways to apply this new knowledge to their daily lives.

CHAPTER 4: Teaching The Zones of Regulation Digital Curriculum

CHECK FOR LEARNING: A quick formative assessment to assess learners' progress toward the concept Learning Targets.

BRIDGE: A summary of each concept to share with others who support learners, including caregivers and support team. Each Bridge includes pertinent concept information and visuals, as well as a fun activity to support generalization.

ZONES VISUALS: Bring The Zones to life in your setting with these visuals that reinforce and extend key Zones concepts.

Universal Design for Learning (UDL)

During the design of *The Zones Digital Curriculum,* we worked closely with CAST, a nonprofit education research and development organization leader in inclusive education that created the Universal Design for Learning framework and UDL Guidelines. Like CAST, we believe that all learners deserve access to high-quality, equitable educational resources that offer meaningful and challenging learning opportunities. We strive to ensure that learners from all backgrounds, economic statuses, or circumstances, as well as those with disabilities, can engage with all of our content and visuals and find their learning inclusive and engaging.

UNIVERSAL DESIGN FOR LEARNING (UDL) GUIDELINES: The UDL Guidelines are a tool used in the implementation of Universal Design for Learning. These guidelines offer a set

---

UNIVERSAL DESIGN FOR LEARNING

Affective networks:
THE **WHY** OF LEARNING

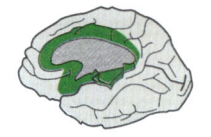

How learners get engaged and stay motivated. How they are challenged, excited, or interested. These are affective dimensions.

- Stimulate interest and motivation for learning

Recognition networks:
THE **WHAT** OF LEARNING

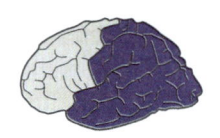

How we gather facts and categorize what we see, hear, and read. Identifying letters, words, or an author's style are recognition tasks.

- Present information and content in different ways

Strategic networks:
THE **HOW** OF LEARNING

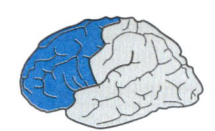

Planning and performing tasks. How we organize and express our ideas. Writing an essay or solving a math problem are strategic tasks.

- Differentiate the ways that students can express what they know

© 2018 CAST, Inc. Used with permission. All rights reserved.

of concrete suggestions that can be applied to any discipline or domain to ensure that all learners can access and participate in meaningful, challenging learning opportunities.

CONCEPT GUIDE PREVIEW

In the following pages, we peek into a Concept Guide and walk through the key parts of a concept. We highlight accessibility and UDL features that not only support access for learners, but also scaffold learning opportunities to engage them. In this chapter, we will further explain and expand upon features you see in this Concept Guide Preview.

INTRODUCTION AND HOOK

Key Vocabulary
Perspective: A person's unique way of feeling, viewing, or thinking about something.
Situation: What is happening at a certain time or place.

INSTRUCTIONS
Preview and post vocabulary as needed.
Use this pre-teaching vocabulary routine:
- Say each word aloud in call and response.
- Access prior knowledge: What do you think the word _____ means? How have you heard it used before?
- Share the definitions on the back of the cards.
- Share the following sentences:
  — My perspective is that summer is the best season.
  — I was in a bad situation. My tire was flat. I did not have a pump. It was dark and no one was around.
- Show the icon and discuss how it relates to the vocabulary

> A best practice routine for introducing key vocabulary supports all, including emergent and multi-lingual learners. Additional vocabulary scaffolds appear throughout each lesson.

> A hook builds interest, activates background knowledge, and engages learners.

Let's Play 4 Corners

Directions: Notice where the four colors are placed in the room. Move to the color that matches your choice for each question.

Which pet would you want?
Dog (blue), Snake (green), Cat (yellow), Fish (red)

How would you like to spend an afternoon? At the park (blue), At the movies (green), At the zoo (yellow), With a book (red)

How would you like to get to and from school?
Bike (blue), Limousine (green), Race Car (yellow), Horse (red)

INSTRUCTIONS
1. Post a green, yellow, red, and blue piece of construction paper in each corner of the room. Be sure that your learners have space to safely move between corners.
2. Share the 4 Corners directions on the slide.

CHAPTER 4: Teaching The Zones of Regulation Digital Curriculum

CORE LESSON

What Animal is This?
Click the + to see different **perspectives**.
It's a duck! It's a bunny!

INSTRUCTIONS
Before clicking the +, have learners vote if they think the image is a duck or a bunny.
- To encourage active participation, have learners answer the question with their hands or body (thumbs up/thumbs down, stand up/sit down).
- Encourage learners to use this sentence stem: *My perspective is ...*
- Remind learners that just as in the Hook activity, there is no right or wrong answer.

Deeper Learning: Make a connection to both fiction and nonfiction texts in which characters and authors have multiple perspectives. For example, a classic fairy tale told from two different points of views or an opinion section where writers debate a topic.

- Images and text from each slide are included for leaders to preview before teaching.
- Suggested engagement activities vary the way learners respond to make learning more interactive, collaborative, and fun.
- Leaders can customize the delivery of the Interactive Presentation (Smartboard, tablet, desktop, etc.) to work best for their setting.
- Slides include photos, animations, and/or scenarios to facilitate comprehension and bring concepts to life.
- Teaching Tips, Scaffolded Learning, and Deeper Learning suggestions provide more ways to support learners across a developmental continuum.

Zones Review: Guess the Feeling
Use the clues to guess the feeling.

Name this Red Zone feeling that starts with A. (Answer: angry)

INSTRUCTIONS
Support learners in guessing the feelings, as needed, by modeling facial expression or providing a scenario where one might experience this emotion. Type in the response, noting that spelling counts. You can play this game more than once, and some of the emotions will randomize in successive plays.

Scaffolding Learning: Review the Zones of Regulation posters created in C2 prior to playing the game. Provide clues to help learners guess the various feelings, as needed.

Alternative Activity: Zones Charades: Cut out the Illustrated Emotions and place them face down in a pile or basket. Have one learner at a time select an emotion and demonstrate it with their facial expressions and body language. Have the other learners guess the feeling and name which Zone it goes in.

- Interactive games and activities build understanding and engagement.
- Alternative Activities offer a non-digital option to further support differentiation and learning preferences.
- Group Activities support learners to synthesize knowledge and apply it to their lives.

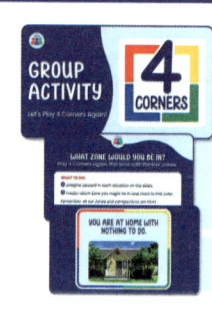

GROUP ACTIVITY — 4 CORNERS

Group Activity
Let's Play 4 Corners Again!

What Zone Would You Be In?
Play 4 Corners again, this time with the four Zones.

What To Do:
1. Imagine yourself in each situation on the slides.
2. Predict which Zone you might be in and move to that color.

Remember, all our Zones and perspectives are OKAY.

Imagine if ...
- You are at home with nothing to do.

Getting Into The **Zones** of Regulation

Pair & Share
Was there a **situation** when you and your partner chose different Zones?

How were your **perspectives** different?

INSTRUCTIONS
Divide learners into pairs. Prompt them to think about the situations from the Group Activity. If needed, click through the situations. Remind learners that everyone has different perspectives and that's OKAY.

Scaffolding Learning: Encourage learners to use the following sentence stems:
- I would be in the (Blue, Green, Yellow, Red) Zone in the following situation ...
- Our perspectives are (the same, different) because ...

> Pair & Share facilitates active participation, develops communication skills, and builds community.

> Sentence starters model the language to talk about feelings and emotions.

> Most concepts include short videos that provide multi-modal learning, which caters to many learners' learning preferences.

All the Zones are Okay, But Not All Behaviors Are
We have learned that all our Zones are okay, but what about our **behavior**?

VIDEO SCRIPT
All our feelings and Zones matter!
Even though all our feelings are okay, not all our actions are.
Our behavior is how we act.
We have many healthy behaviors that help us.
But sometimes when we have strong feelings, our behavior can be unsafe or hurtful to ourselves or others.
For example, it's okay to feel overwhelmed in the Yellow Zone, but it's hurtful to say mean words.
It's okay to feel angry in the Red Zone, but it's not safe to hit or shove someone.
It's okay to feel upset in the Blue Zone, but it's not safe to hurt yourself.
Learning to notice and regulate our Zones also helps us feel more in control of our behavior.

INSTRUCTIONS
Before playing the video, review the difference between feelings and behaviors from Concept 1.
After you watch the video, reinforce that it is okay to have feelings but not okay to act in unsafe or hurtful ways.

WRAP UP

Let's Review
Are all our feelings and Zones okay? (Yes, all our feelings are okay. We can expect to move through all the Zones.)

Is there a difference between our Zone and our behavior? (Yes, our Zone is how we feel on the inside. Our behavior is how we act on the outside. No matter our Zone, we must try to be safe.)

Is it okay to have different perspectives in the same situation? (Yes, we will each have our own perspective in a situation.)

INSTRUCTIONS
Ask the review questions one at a time, inviting learners to share each answer (verbally, journal, or in pairs).

Consider having learners choral read the answers or have learners volunteer to read and/or answer each question.

> Let's Review helps learners self-assess and reflect on key concepts.

> Check for Learning provides a quick formative assessment to monitor learner understanding.

> Alternative Formative Assessments provide differentiation options for learners at varying developmental stages

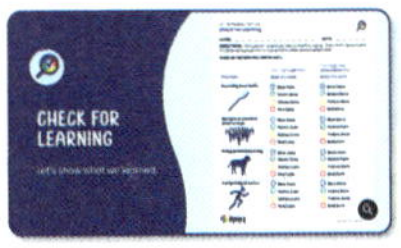

Check for Learning
Let's show what we learned.

INSTRUCTIONS
- Distribute the C3 Check for Learning.
- Enlarge the handout and read aloud the directions. Support learners to complete the activity as independently as possible so it reliably assesses their understanding.

Alternative Formative Assessments:
- **1:1 Task-based:** Share the situations in the C3 Check for Learning and ask the learner to say or indicate the colored Zone they (and a person they know well) might connect with each one.
- **Open-ended question prompts:**
  – Describe a day when you were in all four Zones.
  – Describe a situation when you had a different perspective than someone else.

CHAPTER 4: Teaching The Zones of Regulation Digital Curriculum

HOW TO IMPLEMENT *THE ZONES OF REGULATION DIGITAL CURRICULUM*

As discussed in Chapter 2, teaching The Zones involves a lot more than putting up visuals and suggesting learners regulate with a tool. To teach The Zones of Regulation with fidelity, we recommend the following exposure for learners as a best practice:

- **MINIMUM** of 4 months devoted to teaching and reinforcing the concepts from *The Zones Digital Curriculum*
- **MINIMUM** 40 minutes of direct instruction per concept (can be spread out over a week or more)
- **ONGOING** exposure to the Essential Elements for a Zones Climate

INSTRUCTION GUIDELINES

Teaching, practicing, and reinforcing the concepts and competencies within *The Zones of Regulation® Digital Curriculum* happens in two ways:

1. Direct Instruction

Set aside time each week, based on your implementation schedule, to teach, practice, and/or reinforce Zones Concepts. Instruction ideally happens proactively when learners are in more regulated states where they can focus, engage, and absorb the information. Teaching with fidelity includes:

- Leader following each Concept Guide to structure and sequence instruction
- Teaching the Interactive Presentation (or the suggested off-screen adaptations found in the Concept Guide) for each concept
- Facilitating the Group Activity for each concept, as well as supplementing with appropriate Geared Activities
- Using the accompanying resources for each concept, including the Bridge, Check for Learning, and Zones Visuals
- Reviewing previously taught concepts, visuals, and vocabulary to check for understanding and support generalization

2. Zones Climate

Create and build the Zones Climate using the five Essential Elements discussed in Chapter 3:

1. Provide direct instruction and practice opportunities (as outlined on the left)
2. Post Zones Visuals (after teaching Concept 2)
3. Offer Zones Check-Ins (after teaching Concept 5)
4. Easy access to regulation tools (after teaching Concept 7)
5. Use Zones language

The Zones Climate practices extend beyond the instructional period, being embedded in the environment throughout the day, week, and year.

PACING EACH CONCEPT

Concepts within *The Zones Digital Curriculum* are designed to be taught during multiple sessions so learners have time to explore, practice, and apply what they are learning. Below, we suggest how a concept may be broken down into multiple sessions. Please note that pacing is flexible and should be guided by learners' understanding. Ultimately you, as the leader, should determine what is best for your learners. Each concept can be paced differently, for example, by devoting more time to the Core Lesson or Group Activity. Use the Concept Planner (Appendix, page 137) to help you organize and track your instruction.

Concept Planner

TEACHING A ZONES CONCEPT OVER MULTIPLE 10- TO 15-MINUTE SESSIONS

	Session 1	Session 2	Session 3	Session 4	Session 5
Hook	X				
Core		X			
Group Activity			X		
Geared Activity				X	
Wrap-up Check for Learning					X
The Zones Climate (ongoing)	X	X	X	X	X

TEACHING A ZONES CONCEPT OVER TWO 30-MINUTE SESSIONS

	Session 1	Session 2
Hook	X	
Core	X	
Group Activity	X	
Geared Activity		X
Wrap-up Check for Learning		X
The Zones Climate (ongoing)	X	X

CHAPTER 4: Teaching The Zones of Regulation Digital Curriculum

Recommendations for Concept Pacing

Observe how learners apply the concepts and demonstrate knowledge in everyday situations, before moving on to a new concept that may include more complex/advanced skills and content and/or prerequisite knowledge. For example, if learners are challenged by checking-in in Concept 5: The Zones Check-In, continue building self-awareness and revisit Concept 4: My Signals, My Zones to explore more signals associated with different Zone feelings.

- You may find it useful to break down some concepts even further and teach them over several weeks. For example:
  - With "Concept 2: Introducing The Zones of Regulation," after teaching the Hook in one session, break the Core Lesson into four sessions, using each session to introduce one of the four Zones.
  - Or, for "Concept 4: My Signals, My Zones," after teaching the Hook in one session and the Core Lesson in one session, break apart the Group Activity into four mini-sessions, using each session to teach signals for one Zone.
- Use the suggestions in the Keep It Real! section of the Interactive Presentation, the Geared Activities, and the Zones Climate to help learners grasp the concept and meaningfully apply it to their lives.

PACING THE CURRICULUM

We recommend that concepts be taught in order, as each concept builds upon skills acquired in the prior concepts. Teaching the 10 concepts, at a minimum, should span 4 months, spending roughly at least a week on each concept. It is not necessary to teach a new

IMPORTANT TIP: Learning how to regulate is a process with many moving parts that takes time, patience, understanding, and supportive relationships. The length of time it will take for learners to learn to regulate with more ease will vary greatly, with some able to move through the concepts in weeks and generalize them into daily life with little effort. For other learners, it may be a much longer journey. It is okay to take a break from the curriculum if learners aren't able to grasp the concept introduced or demonstrate their knowledge. With time comes increasing maturity and additional cognitive growth, possibly putting learners in a better place after a hiatus. During a break, you can continue to expose them to Zones Climate Practices, reinforcing and helping them apply concepts they have already learned.

concept every week. Moving too fast through the curriculum can cause learners to shut down, feel unsuccessful, and oppose doing anything "Zones" related. We never want The Zones to become a trigger for learners, leading them to a dysregulated state.

SPIRALING INSTRUCTION

Spiraling is reinforcing previously learned concepts for learners. This leads to better long-term mastery of information, skills, and concepts. Spiraling helps learners make and keep connections over time, which creates more robust pathways for recalling information.

Spiraling Within the Instructional Period

Though we recommend you teach the Zones Concepts in order, we also recommend spiraling back to previously taught concepts to revisit skills throughout an instructional period (such as a school year). Spiraling Zones Concepts can look like any of the following examples:

- After teaching "Concept 4: My Signals, My Zones," revisit "Concept 2: Introducing The Zones of Regulation," to explore and expand emotional vocabulary within the four Zones.

- After teaching "Concept 5: The Zones Check-In," revisit "Concept 4: My Signals, My Zones," to identify new body signals.

- After teaching "Concept 8: Building My Zones Toolbox," revisit "Concept 6: Situations that Trigger and Spark," to identify new triggers and sparks.

- After teaching "Concept 10: The Zones of Regulation Pathway," revisit "Concept 8: Building My Zones Toolbox," to refine and expand the tools in your toolboxes.

- Updating visuals over the scope of instruction

Spiraling Over the Years

The Zones of Regulation is designed as a multi-grade curriculum, and it is expected that concepts will be revisited across grades. Given that The Zones of Regulation integrates a metacognitive system to think about regulation, this system must be refreshed in the learner's memory. For example, every subsequent year, review "Concept 2: Introducing The Zones of Regulation" while also growing the number of emotions associated with each Zone in the new Zones Visuals you construct.

The following concepts are essential to review annually, in order to re-establish the Zones Climate, update learner supports (such as Me

Spiraling examples

CHAPTER 4: Teaching The Zones of Regulation Digital Curriculum

and My Zones Booklet and Zones Toolbox), and apply learning developed over time:

- "Concept 2: Introducing The Zones of Regulation," adding further emotional vocabulary
- "Concept 4: My Signals, My Zones," adding new body signals associated with emotions
- "Concept 5: The Zones Check-In," finding deeper awareness of feelings and signals
- "Concept 6: Situations that Trigger and Spark," expanding awareness as learners develop
- "Concept 8: Building My Zones Toolbox," exploring new tools as learners develop and environments change
- "Concept 10: The Zones of Regulation Pathway," deepening application of the pathway to life experiences

You may opt to teach more concepts than those listed above. The flexibility built into each concept's Geared Activities allows you to revisit content, while offering new activities and ways to explore skills.

Within each concept, the leader has choices in how to best revisit the content. For example, in the figure below, leaders in lower grades review a concept's Interactive Presentation with learners, and then select varied Geared Activities to explore the same learning targets

CONCEPT 2: INTRODUCING THE ZONES OF REGULATION
(AN ESSENTIAL CONCEPT TO REVIEW ANNUALLY)

	Grade 1	Grade 2	Grade 3	Grade 4	Grade 5
Interactive Presentation	C2 Full Presentation	C2 Full Presentation	C2 Full Presentation	C2 Video and related Pair & Share *only*	C2 Video and Pair & Share *question as a journal prompt*
Group Activity	Zones Poster	Zones Poster	Zones Poster	Zones Poster	Zones Poster
Geared Activities	Gear 1: My Zones Poster	Gear 1: Identify Zones in Books and Videos	Gear 2: Zones Bingo	Gear 2: Guess the Emotion	Gear 3: Make a Playlist

with a different level of support and depth, supporting learners to apply skills over time as they grow. In the upper grades, only the video and *Pair & Share* are used from the Interactive Presentation. Spiraling through The Zones will also re-establish the Zones Climate in your setting each year.

Sample Grade-Level Alignment Chart: If aligning Zones instruction over multiple years and grade levels, consider creating a detailed plan that identifies activities to use with various developmental levels. See example below in the Geared Activities section.

HOW TO TEACH A CONCEPT

Follow these steps to successfully teach each concept.

CONCEPT PREPARATION CHECKLIST

- [ ] Read the Concept Guide: What and Why, Instructional Plan, and Zones Climate. You may choose to highlight and bookmark certain pages/sections within the platform.
- [ ] Preview the Interactive Presentation, referring to the Concept Guide for support and teaching tips.
- [ ] Print needed core resources for learners (Group Activity, Check for Learning, Zones Bridge).
- [ ] Select and print applicable Zones Visuals for use in your setting.
- [ ] Select (and print if necessary) at least one Geared Activity for learners.
- [ ] Gather materials for the Group Activity and/or Geared Activities.
- [ ] Adapt materials to best suit your learners.
- [ ] Gather optional More Zones Resources to support and extend learning.

USING THE INTERACTIVE PRESENTATION

We know that instruction is most meaningful and impactful when learners are actively engaged in the learning process. Therefore, we've designed a digital Interactive Presentation that integrates several features to engage learners with the content:

- Games and interactives
- Pair & Share prompts
- Videos

CHAPTER 4: Teaching The Zones of Regulation Digital Curriculum

- Engaging images and animation
- Movement activities

We recommend that you don't just read the slide content and have learners passively observe, but rather follow suggestions in the Concept Guide to encourage learner participation in different ways with specific slides.

INTERACTIVE ACTIVITY EXAMPLES

SORT THE TOOLS — Think about each tool. Which Zone might it help YOU regulate? This will be different for each person. Select a 👆 to choose the Zone you might be in when you use this tool.

DRAWING OR COLORING

Learners sort a tool into its matching Zone.

[Image: phone screen showing a child covering ears, captioned "It's too noisy in the room." with Trigger / Spark buttons, 8/8 Finish]

Learners classify situations as Triggers or Sparks.

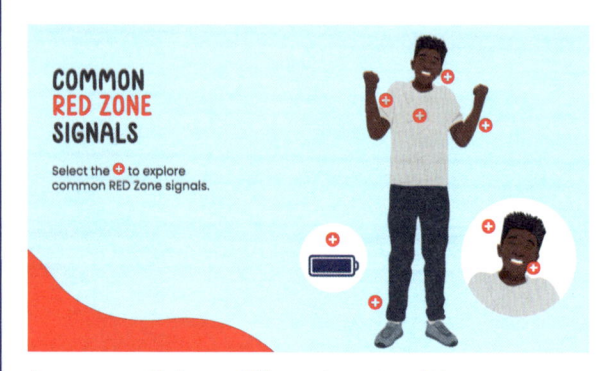

COMMON RED ZONE SIGNALS — Select the ⊕ to explore common RED Zone signals.

Learners click on different parts of the body to explore Red Zone signals.

Recommendations for Engaging Learners Throughout an Interactive Presentation

- Have volunteer learners take turns reading slide content aloud.

- Pause to have learners make connections to the content. Encourage different non-verbal signals to volunteer information, such as giving a thumbs-up or down, shaking/nodding head, standing up, etc., to indicate if they agree or disagree with the content.

- For interactive slide activities, learners can take turns making choices directly on the digital device or board (if using a Smartboard).

- Learners chorally say responses aloud at the same time (best used for one-word or very short answers).

- Embed movement into learning, such as when a learner wants to share a response, they are invited to stand and share it; or designate different parts of the room that learners can move to for multiple choice or voting options.

- After asking a question, the leader picks from a group of class craft sticks, each of which has a learner's name on it. The chosen learner answers the question or chooses to pass it on to the next learner. Stick selection can continue until a sufficient number of answers are heard.

- Most slides include a visual that relates to the slide content. After sharing the text, have learners Pair & Share about the relationship between the visuals and the text on a slide.

- After a session, pair learners to name three things they learned, two things they found interesting, and one question they still have.
- For videos:
  - Show it multiple times, each time asking learners to ponder a specific question or look for specific details.
  - When watching, turn off the sound. Watch in silence to get curious or gather initial evidence that might help answer a focus question, then watch again with sound to find out which questions get answered.

DIFFERENTIATE WITH GEARED ACTIVITIES

The Geared Activities, found within each concept, are designed to differentiate and deepen the instruction for a wide variety of learners using the Universal Design for Learning (UDL) Guidelines (referenced earlier in this chapter). Use these varied activities following the Group Activity (in the Core Lesson section of the Interactive Presentation) to provide learners the opportunity to practice, apply, and extend learning through multiple learning modalities (see Geared Activity Learning Preferences Key).

The Geared Activities found within each concept are divided into three different gears that offer differentiated levels of support. **Please note that a gear is a type of activity, NOT a type of learner.** Depending on a learner's strengths, goals, and skills, they may benefit from activities within multiple gears, or you may vary gears depending on the concept.

Deciding Which Geared Activity Is Right for Your Learners

The gear you select for your learners is flexible and will likely differ depending on the content. Choose a Geared Activity based on:

- Prior knowledge and language
- Strengths and interests
- Accessibility: Where is this learner on the developmental continuum for this skill?

You may choose to do multiple activities within one gear with your learners, or jump from one gear to the next, depending on how much practice and reinforcement learners need within a particular concept. Geared Activities are designed to be flexible!

GEARED ACTIVITY LEARNING PREFERENCES KEY

- Acting
- Art
- Data
- Digital Group Activity
- Game
- Graphic Organizer
- Literature Connection
- Movement
- Music
- Presentation
- Search
- Technology
- Writing

CHAPTER 4: Teaching The Zones of Regulation Digital Curriculum

AN OVERVIEW OF GEARED ACTIVITIES

	Gear 1	Gear 2	Gear 3
Purpose	Designed to support **early emergent** regulation development and strengthen language strategies. These activities are the most concrete, visual, and heavily supported by adult facilitators.	Designed to support **intermediate regulation** development. Activities help learners meaningfully apply the learning targets to their individual lives.	Designed to support more **metacognitive regulation** development, building agency, and independent application of the learning targets.
Who It's For	Consider for younger learners 5–7 years of age and learners with intellectual disabilities or divergent social emotional learning abilities.	Consider for primary-/elementary-age learners (7–12 years of age) and older learners needing more support with social emotional learning and regulation.	Consider for adolescent and adult learners or older elementary-age learners who have had repeated exposure to The Zones of Regulation curriculum content in previous years and can demonstrate understanding.
Instruction Approach	All leader-led including a mix of independent and group activities	Variety of leader-led and learner-led activities that offer a mix of independent and group activities	• All learner-led activities, presented in a choice menu to appeal to a variety of learners • Mix of independent and group activities • Activities designed for agency and choice that relate to social context and well-being
Activity features may include:	• Simple emotional vocabulary • Little to no independent writing or reading • Concrete and hands-on activities • Structured, Box Task approach: Velcro, sort, match, clothes pin	• Moderate emotion vocabulary • Some independent reading and writing (limited to sentence writing with word/idea prompts) • Use creative expression (draw, write, construct) to explore concepts and skills • More application and drawing conclusions than Gear 1	• Use extended emotion vocabulary • Independent readers and writers (can write paragraphs, narratives, journals, etc.) • Incorporates metacognition-contextualizing skills and real-life application • Synthesis and representation, show learning your own way

ADAPT FOR LEARNERS

The Zones of Regulation is highly adaptable, allowing you the flexibility to make it the most pertinent and relatable to your learners. What always remains fixed are the four Zones and what they represent, as well as how our tools help us regulate our Zones. What can vary, for example, is the depth to which the concepts are applied, the varied visuals that speak to your learner, how you make it accessible, the extent you use language to reinforce concepts, etc. No two leaders implement The Zones exactly the same way, nor should they, as they would not be considering their learners—their needs, strengths, abilities, interests, and experiences. Luckily, the Digital Curriculum makes it easy for you to follow the curriculum scope and sequence, while also allowing you to modify the content and adapt your delivery to make it the right fit for your learners.

We encourage you to use your judgment for differentiating, adapting, and scaffolding the content found within the concepts. After all, YOU are the expert for your learners, not us. In addition to selecting the Geared Activities, you may find you need to further adapt or customize how concepts are presented depending on your learner's age, language, development, lived experiences, authentic goals, and abilities. Suggestions are provided throughout the Concept Guide to support this.

Considerations

- **LEARNERS WITH INTELLECTUAL DISABILITIES AND EMERGENT COMMUNICATION SKILLS:** These learners may not develop a deep understanding and application of all concepts within The Zones, because of its metacognitive structure and language-based strategies. Yet with consistent exposure, access to visual supports, and opportunities for practice, many can gain awareness of their feelings and Zones and increase their communication around regulation. Learners may become more open to co-regulation cues and supports through using The Zones. Each Concept Guide contains several accessibility and adaptation suggestions for learners with emergent regulation skills.

- **LEARNERS IN THE MIDST OF A MENTAL HEALTH CRISIS:** These learners need stabilization before The Zones of Regulation is introduced as an intervention. Connecting with wrap-around services is a top priority.

CHAPTER 4: Teaching The Zones of Regulation Digital Curriculum

- **LEARNERS WITH IDENTIFIED REGULATION DIFFERENCES (INCLUDING AUTISM, ADHD, ETC.):** Use of The Zones curriculum should not be thought of as a "quick fix" to help these learners stop a challenging behavior, but rather as a teaching tool to use gradually over time to support them in their ongoing regulation learning journey. Be aware that these learners may still demonstrate dysregulated and/or challenging behaviors. Rather than replacing existing positive behavior support plans, The Zones concepts and strategies can be woven into these plans as learners and the adults who support them gain awareness of a learner's strengths, goals, and unique needs. As you progress through The Zones curriculum and build a common language around feelings and coping strategies, you may also integrate Zones language and concepts in restorative and problem-solving conversations, when the learner is ready to process a situation.

- **LEARNERS WHO HAVE EXPERIENCED TRAUMA:** The Zones can be a very effective intervention for these learners once a strong, trusting relationship has been established with the leader and there is sensitivity to the unique needs of the learner. It may be painful or difficult for these learners to identify their feelings and Zone as they may experience emotional detachment and have a difficult time connecting with the physical sensations associated with feelings. There are trauma-informed care tips and considerations that pertain to each concept in the Concept Guide.

Zones in Individualized Learning Plans

As you approach instruction with learners who have regulation needs identified in individualized plans such as Individualized Education Plans (IEPs), Section 504 Intervention Plans, treatment plans, or Positive Behavior Support Plans (Behavior Intervention Plans), the Zones may be used as a method or intervention and can be important for providing targeted instruction. However, we discourage you from naming The Zones or including Zones-specific language into the goals. Goals should center around growing competencies in regulation and social emotional learning, not mastery of The Zones concepts. It is important to consider access to visuals, language prompts/cues, triggers (and sparks), and regulation tools when creating support plans as a road map for supportive adults to follow to best co-regulate with a particular learner.

For sample regulation goals, see Appendix, page 138, Sample Individualized Regulation Goals.

Overlaying The Zones with Other SEL Resources

The Zones of Regulation curriculum can easily be adapted and woven together with other social emotional learning (SEL) curriculum and practices, such as comprehensive SEL curricula, restorative practices, and programs that address sensory integration, mindfulness, yoga, character building/growth mindset, and conflict resolution skills. For example, when learning about yoga poses, present them as regulation tools and have learners sort them into the Zones they help regulate; or when learning about growth mindset, connect The Zones to the various thinking patterns explored. When implementing The Zones, you create a common language and healthy climate while building a metacognitive approach to regulation that can serve as a strong foundation to use with a wide range of other SEL resources. When implementing other programs consider the following steps:

- Teach the four Signature Practices and utilize Essential Elements of a Zones Climate as a foundation (Chapter 2 and 3).
- Map out strengths, overlaps, and unique characteristics of each program.
- Develop an implementation plan detailing pacing for layered instruction.

EXTEND LEARNING

This section found at the end of each Concept Guide offers ideas and strategies to support learners in applying, generalizing, and extending the skills taught beyond your core instruction. It includes the following sections:

The Zones Climate

As discussed in Chapter 3, establishing a safe climate that promotes well-being is foundational to the environment where we teach The Zones. To enhance the climate, each concept includes a Zones Climate section that provides suggestions on how to integrate key concepts into the learner's environment, further establishing this is a safe space to talk about and care for our feelings. Collectively, the suggestions found in this section are integral in formulating what we refer to as the Zones Climate.

CHAPTER 4: Teaching The Zones of Regulation Digital Curriculum

Example of a Zones Bridge from Concept 1 in The Zones of Regulation Digital Curriculum

Bridging The Zones: Connect with Supportive Adults

Although collaboration among team members can seem cumbersome, it is critical for learners' success. In all settings, having team members (leaders, caregivers, classroom assistants, therapists, counselors, administrators, and support staff) on board and familiar with The Zones concepts and terms creates a comfortable and supportive environment for learners to effectively practice their regulation skills. To simplify this for leaders, each concept includes easy-to-distribute information that we call the Zones Bridge. Each Bridge includes the following sections: What Are We Learning?, Why Is It Important?, Ask and Share (discussion questions), and a quick activity to reinforce the concept. In addition, research has shown (Miranda, Presentación, and Soriano, 2002 and Sofronoff, 2005) neurodivergent individuals make more gains when the caregivers and leaders share resources and strategies to support the learners.

When possible, set aside time to connect with caregivers and staff who work closely with the learner(s) to establish the terminology, concepts, strategies, and practices that can support them. Explain to supportive adults the value of reinforcing Zones concepts throughout daily life in a variety of settings. This prepares adults to help the learner co-regulate, orient them to Zones Visuals, and to find tools to support regulating their Zone without having to "manage the behavior."

As concepts are completed, copies of completed handouts can be sent home in addition to the Zones Bridge. We stress copies as it is best to keep the originals so learners can spiral back to the concept later in the curriculum and build upon their knowledge. Also provide relevant copies for other supportive adults on their team, or who work closely with the learner, who would benefit from being informed. For example, a learner who may frequently feel dysregulation on the bus would benefit from the bus driver being in the know and having a copy of the learner's toolbox to reference. Keeping communication open among all team members provides the learner with ongoing support as they move through the curriculum.

More Zones Resources

This section includes optional ancillary Zones of Regulation products and materials that support, reinforce, and/or extend the concept's core instruction. These adjunctive Zones related resources integrate a variety of mediums to engage learners, such as storybooks, apps, tool cards, posters, and games and deepen learning for different age groups. Following you will find all the Zones related resources referenced throughout *The Zones Digital Curriculum*, plus a brief description and age range:

- *The Zones of Regulation App*: An interactive tool that provides a fun way to assist in developing real-life regulation skills. Learners will be taken on an adventure through a town filled with exciting learning opportunities around Zones concepts, rewards, and mini-games. Currently available for download on iPhone, iPad, Android, Mac, Chromebook (Android compatible). One app download may be used for up to 8 unique learners. (ages 5+ with supportive adult)

- *Exploring Emotions App*: The second app from The Zones, *Exploring Emotions*, is designed to foster regulation skills in an engaging manner, while simulating realistic everyday situations. It helps learners gain skills in consciously regulating their feelings within their environments. Currently available for download on iPhone, iPad, Android, Mac, Chromebook (Android compatible). One app download may be used for up to 26 unique learners. (ages 5+)

- *Navigating The Zones* and *Advanced Pack:* This game is an interactive teaching tool designed to extend the curriculum, giving participants the opportunity to walk through the Zones Pathway. Players should have a strong working knowledge of the concepts and vocabulary in The Zones curriculum to use this product and before advancing to the *Advanced Pack* to extend play. (ages 8+)

- *The Zones of Regulation Poster*: A visual to reinforce the four Zones and the common feelings associated with each, as well as space to add strategies or tools to support regulation of each Zone. (ages 5+)

- *Triggers and Sparks Poster:* Use this poster to brainstorm your triggers and sparks. Noticing them helps us be prepared for when they happen again. This way, we aren't as surprised when our feelings change, and we can regulate and/or problem solve more easily. (ages 5+)

- *STOP, OPT & GO Poster:* This poster supports the decision-making that goes into regulation, while also addressing problem solving and group conflict resolution. First we pause before we act, think about our options and how they may work out, then use our goal to decide on the best option. It also can be used proactively to prepare learners manage themselves when they encounter previously identified triggers. (ages 5+)

- *Zones Check-In Poster:* Use this poster to support learners in mindfully pausing to check in with their body signals, emotions, and Zones. (ages 5+)

- *The Zones Pathway Poster:* Learning culminates in the Digital Curriculum with the Zones Pathway. This poster outlines 5 concrete steps to support regulation, making it accessible for learners to move through in real time. (ages 5+)

- *The Zones of Regulation Storybook Set | The Road to Regulation and The Regulation Station:* This two-storybook set provides engaging social scenarios and strategies to help learners explore how concepts from The Zones curriculum can be used at school and at home. Kids love stories and will identify with the characters and the everyday situations as they learn about their feelings and emotions, as well as how their body helps them sense what they are feeling. (ages 5–11)

- *The Road to Regulation Poster:* Adapted from a colorful 2-page illustration in *The Regulation Station* storybook, this full-color poster outlines the steps along the Road to Regulation (Zones Pathway) taught in The Zones of Regulation Storybook Set. (ages 5+)

- *Tools to Try Cards: The Zones Tools to Try Cards for Kids* (ages 5–10) and *Tools to Try Cards for Tweens & Teens* (ages 10+) include over fifty 4"× 6" tool cards. These two separate decks are an easy, user-friendly way to introduce regulation strategies and empower learners to choose tools that work best for them. Each strategy card displays the regulation tool on one side and a how-to-do-it description on the reverse, along with a metacognitive self-reflection.

(All products except the apps are available from Social Thinking: www.socialthinking.com.)

WAYS TO CHECK FOR LEARNING AND MEASURE PROGRESS

There are several data collection tools that Zones leaders can use to assess, measure, and track progress within the Digital Curriculum. Each Concept includes a Check for Learning to gauge learners' mastery of the concept's learning targets. In addition, we suggest using these practices to measure progress while working through concepts:

- Listening for learners' depth of understanding when participating in discussions or showing work
- Looking for insights displayed when completing activities or work
- Direct observation of skills being applied
- Listening for insights from learners and others who work closely with them

In addition, numerous assessment and progress monitoring tools and accompanying information/directions can be found within the Appendix. As a best practice, we recommend that you gather data from different types of assessments, observations, and experiences with a learner to gain a full understanding of their regulation competencies and progress over time.

LEARNER ASSESSMENT TOOLS

Assessment Tool	Type of Assessment	Quick Description
Regulation Self-Reflection (Appendix page 141)	Pre/Mid/Post	Learner self-evaluation of regulation skills and competencies
Observing Regulation Competencies (Appendix page 146)	Pre/Mid/Post	Informal assessment of a learner's regulation skills and competencies by a familiar adult
Check for Learning (Found in each concept)	Progress Monitoring	Leader assesses learner's mastery of learning targets at the end of each concept
Learning Target Rubric (Appendix page 143)	Progress Monitoring	Organizes and tracks progress toward learning targets over the scope of the curriculum
*Observation and Questioning (See below)	Informal	Ongoing assessment of learner's understanding throughout curriculum instruction

OBSERVATION AND QUESTIONING: WHAT TO WATCH FOR

You can informally assess learners by observing their level of engagement in the learning process. It's important to do these ongoing checks throughout each concept. This allows you to see which learners need additional support and which learners have grasped the concept and are ready to move on.

CHAPTER 4: Teaching The Zones of Regulation Digital Curriculum

ZONES CLIMATE AND IMPLEMENTATION ASSESSMENT TOOLS

Assessment Tool	Type of Assessment	Quick Description
The Zones Climate Rubric (Appendix, page 133)	Progress Monitoring	Self-evaluate Zones Climate Elements, set goals, and use as a walk-through observation strategy
Digital Curriculum Implementation & Fidelity Checklist (Appendix, page 148)	Fidelity Observation	Used to assess adherence to curriculum elements and quality of instruction and implementation

For further resources and measures to support assessment and evaluation of regulation competencies, see Appendix, page 128: Assessing Regulation Competencies.

The following are examples of opportunities for such observation:

- Asking questions throughout instruction and activities to gauge understanding

- Response to co-regulation attempts by adults (For example, a staff may offer, "Let's go check your Zone," and the learner is willing; or a staff offers a learner their toolbox visuals, and learner selects one to try.)

- Listening to learners' contributions in discussion or reading their journal entries (For example, consider learners' ability to relate to concepts by providing personal examples and meaningfully applying concepts to their life. Make sure to note the accuracy of their responses and self-reporting compared to what is observed through their behavior. Often learners don't give themselves enough credit and are overly hard on themselves.)

- Tracking observable learner data, such as time spent on task, time spent in the classroom, number of conflicts involving staff intervention, office referrals/suspensions, behavior prompts from staff, frequency of dysregulated disruptive behavior, duration of dysregulated behavior, etc.

- Reviewing completed activities and asking questions or giving prompts such as, "Tell me more about your body signals in the Yellow Zone."

CHECK FOR LEARNING

Each concept within the Digital Curriculum contains a printable Check for Learning, which is a short formative assessment to measure learners' progress toward the Learning Targets. These assessments are meant to be quick, asking learners to fill in the blank, draw, label, or answer short questions. Within each Concept Guide, you will also find two ways to adapt the Check for Learning to best fit your learners and setting:

- 1:1 Task-based: Performance tasks that can be used to assess understanding in a one-on-one format, do not require learners to independently read or write/draw.

- Open-ended question prompts: Alternative questions that can be used as an "exit slip," question of the day, or journal prompt to assess understanding.

Check for Learning assessments are not scored, rather they are designed to provide leaders with a quick and easy way to identify which learners may need additional support and reinforcement and which learners have grasped the concept and are ready to move on.

LEARNER SELF-MONITORING

Learners' completion of self-monitoring activities not only allows adults to gain insights into learners' grasp and application of concepts, but also supports learners in assessing their own ability to apply what they are learning. Self-monitoring activities are integrated throughout the curriculum, such as in Concept 5, you will find the following Geared Activities that incorporate self-monitoring: Floating Through the Zones, Check-In/Check-Out, and Zones Across the Day. Later in the curriculum, learners self-monitor their regulation tools' effectiveness in Concept 8 and their journey on the Zones Pathway in Concept 10.

IMPLEMENT THE ZONES IN DIFFERENT SETTINGS

Implementation of The Zones of Regulation can occur in a variety of settings. There is no best place to implement; in fact, a best practice is for learning to happen across settings. Ultimately, teaching learners in their natural environment, whether it's their home, classroom, or community setting, will help them best connect with their authentic experiences and apply learning.

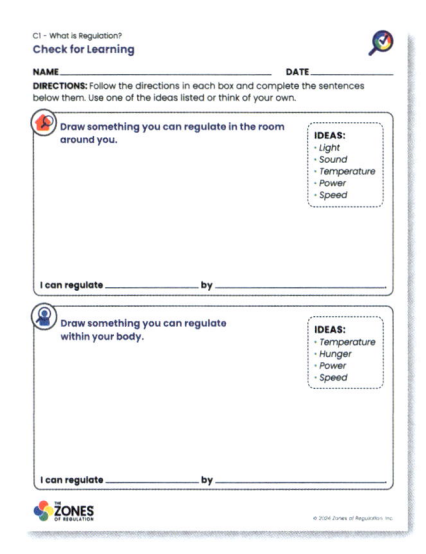

Example of a Check for Learning from Concept 1 in The Zones of Regulation Digital Curriculum

> **DO** expose other adults and learners in the setting to Zones teachings, so everyone can be on the same page, using the same language. This facilitates inclusiveness, equity, and co-regulation.
>
> **DON'T** teach Zones of Regulation to a learner in only a pull-out or 1:1 model without collaborating with other connected adults who can help support the learner across settings.

ROLES TO SUPPORT IMPLEMENTATION

Depending on the implementation plan, there are likely one of two ways that adults are involved with teaching and supporting The Zones of Regulation within a setting:

1. Adults can lead instruction in Zones of Regulation concepts in the setting. When this is your role, we refer to you as the "leader" and you provide direct instruction of The Zones of Regulation curriculum.

2. Adults can reinforce Zones of Regulation instruction that is being led in a different setting (such as in school, therapy or special services, or community organization). In this case, adults can follow along with concepts taught through the Zones Bridge handouts and regular communication with the leader. Your role will involve carrying out the activities and suggestions in the Bridge in your setting to help learners practice and generalize new skills, as well as extending the Zones Climate to your setting.

In either one of these scenarios, your role involves establishing Zones Climate practices in your setting, helping create an environment where talking about and regulating feelings is the norm.

HOME

Extending The Zones of Regulation into the home is so important for learners, as well as caregivers, to develop and support regulation in arguably the most critical setting. For more tips and support on using The Zones in a home setting, please refer to Appendix, page 139, Zones in the Home and consider attending our *Zone Your Home: A Parent/Caregiver Training* (see https://zonesofregulation.com/training/zoneyourhome/).

WHAT CAN THE ZONES LOOK LIKE IN DIFFERENT SETTINGS?

HOME

- Includes residential settings
- Implementing and using Zones Climate Elements
- Some direct instruction of Zones concepts including the Signature Practices
- Bridge: Closely working with educators, therapists, other team members to carry over direct instruction happening in other settings (such as school or therapy)

Refer to the Home section on page 116, as well as *Zones in the Home* (Appendix, page 139).

SCHOOL

- Direct instruction within or across multi-tiered supports (Tier 1, 2, 3)
- Instruction led by school counselors, school social workers, special education staff, general education teachers (depends on implementation plan)
- Zones Climate Elements utilized schoolwide
- Zones is used as an inclusion strategy for learners with regulation differences
- Bridge: Closely working with caregivers, teachers, outside of school providers to carry over direct instruction to other settings

Refer to the Schools and Classroom section on the following pages for further information.

AFTER-SCHOOL & COMMUNITY PROGRAMS

- Includes childcare programs, clubs, community or religious groups, camps, sports, arts programs, etc.
- Implementing and using Zones Climate Elements
- Direct instruction of Zones concepts may vary
- Bridge: Closely working with educators, caregivers, other team members to carry over direct instruction happening in other settings (such as school or therapy)

CLINICAL & THERAPEUTIC PRACTICE

- Includes clinics, hospitals, treatment centers, private centers, and correctional facilities
- Instruction in an individual or small-group format
- Highly personalized goals and treatment plans
- Highly adapted instruction for each individual or group
- Bridge: Closely working with caregivers, educators, and support team to use Zones Climate Elements and help learners apply skills across settings

CHAPTER 4: Teaching The Zones of Regulation Digital Curriculum

SCHOOLS AND CLASSROOMS

The Zones of Regulation has been widely adopted by schools around the world to foster regulation and social emotional learning (SEL) competencies. The Zones can be used in many ways within a school setting, from individually or in small groups by a therapist/counselor, to select classes or grades by a classroom leader or guest leader (e.g., school counselor or OT), to schoolwide where every classroom, as well as all staff, embraces The Zones. In addition to its application in general education classrooms, The Zones of Regulation has proven to be a valuable resource in special education and targeted interventions to provide identified learners more intensive instruction and support around regulation and social emotional learning. This leads to further inclusion and positive outcomes. As you learned in "Chapter 3: Building The Zones Climate," school staff are encouraged to adapt and integrate The Zones into all aspects of a school culture. In addition, The Zones concepts can be woven into academic content throughout the school day, rather than only at a specific time and place (which will be discussed in more detail in this section).

The Zones Across Tiered Instruction

The Zones of Regulation® Digital Curriculum can easily be used within tiered support systems widely adopted in education settings, such as Multi-Tiered Systems of Support (MTSS). When The Zones was first developed, it was primarily used for small-group or individual interventions (Tiers 2 and 3). With the paradigm shift in

ZONES OF REGULATION INSTRUCTION WITHIN MULTI-TIERED SYSTEMS

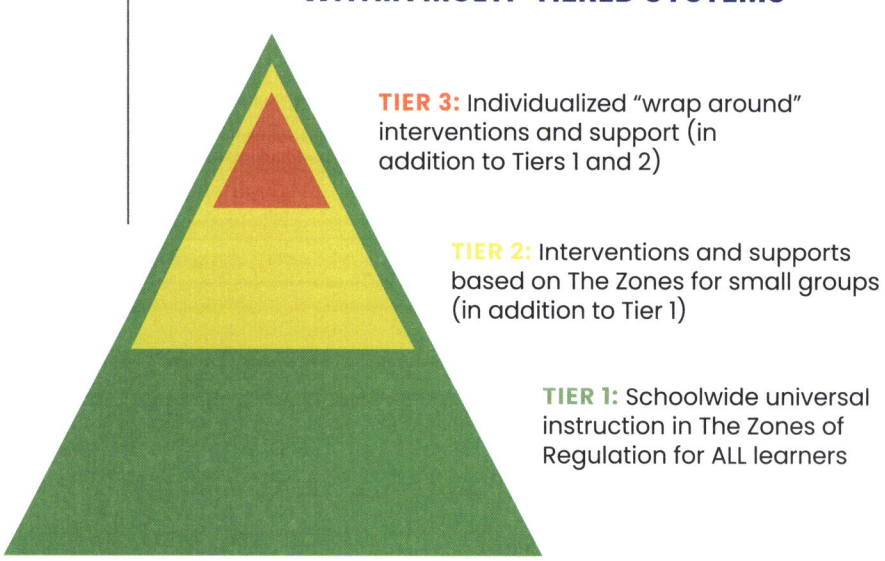

TIER 3: Individualized "wrap around" interventions and support (in addition to Tiers 1 and 2)

TIER 2: Interventions and supports based on The Zones for small groups (in addition to Tier 1)

TIER 1: Schoolwide universal instruction in The Zones of Regulation for ALL learners

MTSS/PBIS AND ZONES OF REGULATION CROSSWALK

	Description	Zones of Regulation Instruction/ Interventions at Each Tier
TIER 1	MTSS: Core Programming PBIS: Universal Prevention Schoolwide programming and direct instruction in social, emotional, and behavioral competencies is provided for all learners. Instruction is proactive, preventive, and universal.	• Zones concepts are taught schoolwide in general education classrooms as positive, proactive instruction to promote regulation, wellness, and inclusion. • Zones of Regulation is used as a common language within the building by all staff and learners, including restorative and problem-solving discussions. • Zones Visuals are found throughout the building. • All learners and leaders are encouraged to participate in Zones Check-Ins as part of their daily routines. • A variety of regulation tools are accessible for both learners and leaders to use across settings. • Caregivers/families provide input and are provided information on The Zones of Regulation framework and how to carry over practices in the home/community.
TIER 2	MTSS: Supplemental Interventions PBIS: Targeted Prevention Interventions are targeted toward learners identified as "at-risk" or needing additional supplement to Tier 1 instruction. This may consist of small group, and/or targeted behavioral or mental health supports.	• Learners with like social, emotional, and/or behavioral goals are grouped for more frequent and targeted instruction of Zones of Regulation concepts. • Differentiated/adapted instruction of Zones content is provided, using the curriculum differentiation features and guidance to match strengths, development, goals, and needs. • More opportunities to practice and apply Zones concepts are embedded throughout the day. • Increased access to individualized tools/strategies is provided. • Increased positive reinforcement around identifying feelings/Zones and using tools to regulate is provided. • Collaboration between home, community settings, and school is provided for consistent use of Zones of Regulation programming across settings.
TIER 3	MTSS: Intensive Intervention PBIS: Intensive, Individualized Prevention Intensified and individualized interventions and "wrap around" support is provided for learners needing additional supplements to both Tier 1 and Tier 2 supports.	• Individualized Zones of Regulation instruction and visual supports tailored to learner's strengths, development, and interests are provided. • More frequent exposure and/or 1:1 instruction and practice around Zones of Regulation concepts is provided. • Trained staff offer additional co-regulation supports. • Learners receive increased access to individualized tools/strategies, as well as frequent practice in using tools when in a calm state. • Increased positive reinforcement around identifying feelings/Zones and using tools to regulate is provided. • Increased consultation between home, school, and outside providers such as therapists is provided. • Individualized positive behavior support plans are developed to guide staff in supporting learner's regulation and well-being.

*NOTE that learners receiving special education services have access to instructional support in any tiers that apply to their unique skills, needs, and goals.

Resources: Multi-Level Prevention System | Center on Multi-Tiered Systems of Support (mtss4success.org) Center on PBIS (pbis.org)

education over the last decade calling for the education of the whole child and support for social emotional learning, we have seen a dramatic increase in schools that are using The Zones in Tier 1. This establishes common language and practices in SEL that can be built upon in Tiers 2 and 3. The Zones of Regulation is a proactive practice or intervention that can be applied at varying intensities within all the differing tiers of support. What is unique about The Zones is that it builds positive mental health and social emotional competencies for all, while serving as an inclusion strategy for neurodivergent learners and learners with trauma histories and regulation differences. It provides the universal language and a visual system that EVERYONE can use in school, home, and even if they move to a new school within the district.

Connect to Academic Standards

Given that we experience feelings across all aspects of the school day, *The Zones of Regulation Digital Curriculum* can be adapted and integrated into teaching of core subjects to address K–12 state academic standards. The following are some examples of how you can connect the lessons/concepts to these standards.

- **Math:** Creating bar/line graphs and pie charts based on data collected from learners during the Zones Check-Ins; constructing and interpreting line and bar graphs, using data to draw conclusions regarding regulation tools to try, and looking for patterns over time

- **Reading/Literature:** Increasing vocabulary around emotions and sensations; using comprehension and inference skills to identify characters' shifting Zones as well as their use of tools/strategies; relating the text to individual learner's prior knowledge and personal experience

- **Writing:** Creating poetry, personal narratives, opinion pieces, and fictional stories that explore feelings, thoughts, and related actions in varying contexts/situations

- **Speaking/Listening:** Communicating effectively through participating in conversations and formal discussions about The Zones concepts; following two-step directions; attending to and understanding the meanings of messages; communicating needs, feelings, and ideas to peers and adults; and using a voice level appropriate for the language situation

- **Social Studies:** Exploring multiple perspectives and the role of emotions within historical and current events

Schoolwide Implementation

When using The Zones for Tier 1 instruction, the implementation process and plan is approached differently at each school. There is no "right" way to roll out *The Zones of Regulation Digital Curriculum*, however, schools that have successfully implemented The Zones schoolwide share four common factors:

1. **Administrator support:** The administrators (and district staff) are involved in planning the implementation of Zones schoolwide. They are included in planning meetings, trainings, and use the Zones Climate Elements in their own spaces. Ultimately, administrators will set the tone for making The Zones an integral and sustained part of a school climate.

2. **Zones champions who take leadership:** This effort is brought forward and supported by staff who have experience supporting wellness, positive mental health, and social emotional learning with their learners. Zones champions are often counselors, social workers, general and/or special education leaders, and therapists (occupational, speech and language).

3. **Staff buy-in:** In addition to understanding how to use The Zones, make sure everyone understands WHY The Zones can help and what problems it can solve. Consider piloting The Zones in a few classes first and having staff share their success stories to build confidence, enthusiasm, and momentum before launching schoolwide.

4. **An implementation plan:** Create an implementation plan that identifies how instruction will be rolled out in the first year and beyond. Identify the implementation process in detail including the who, what, when, and how of training staff, teaching the lessons, and collecting data.

Zones Connection: Schoolwide Implementation Resources

For further information and resources for Schoolwide Zones Implementation visit https://zonesofregulation.com/for-your-school/.

Zones Champions consider attending Tier-1 Team Training (see https://zonesofregulation.com/training/tier-1-team-training/).

CHAPTER 4: Teaching The Zones of Regulation Digital Curriculum

> **WHAT THE ZONES OF REGULATION IS AND ISN'T**
>
> | The Zones IS | The Zones ISN'T |
> |---|---|
> | • A proactive, skills-based approach | • A behavior approach or a punitive discipline model |
> | • A simple, common language to understand, talk about, and teach regulation | • A system for projecting shame, judgment, or suppression of feelings |
> | • A consistent, metacognitive pathway to follow for regulation and well-being | • A scripted curriculum with different lessons for each age/grade level |
> | • A systematic framework with a developmental sequence of concepts and lessons | • Only about teaching the four Zones and feelings associated with them |
> | • Flexible, meant to be adapted for your learners and setting | • A "one size fits all" framework |

CONCLUSION

The content in *Getting Into The Zones* has spanned numerous topics and delved into strategies to support the growth of regulation and social emotional competencies for both you and your learners. I'd like to use a gardening analogy to frame this information.

As you set up a garden, you consider the conditions such as the soil, weather, and sunlight, and expand your understanding of what helps your plants grow. These are similar to the elements we discussed in Chapter 1—understanding regulation and considering *what is under the hood* as well as *what's the terrain* for your learners.

In Chapter 2, we discussed the framework and Signature Practices of The Zones of Regulation—the four Zones, the Zones Check-In, the Zones Toolbox, and the Zones Pathway—these are the seeds or the base of your garden. Also, the Zones Key Principles introduced in Chapter 2 can be thought of as the roots that take hold to strengthen your planting efforts.

Like fertilizer, the Zones Climate (discussed in Chapter 3) enhances growth by creating a safe, inclusive, supportive environment focused on well-being where experiencing feelings and regulating is the norm, not the exception.

Lastly, none of this growth is possible without the essential elements or nutrients to grow—sun and water. *The Zones of Regulation Digital Curriculum* (outlined in this chapter) provides the Essential Elements and nutrients for your learners to flourish and thrive. Though the four Zones and the Zones Pathway are intentionally simple—like the seeds—we can't just plant them and expect they will be able to grow. All the concepts in *The Zones Digital Curriculum* scaffold learning so that learners can make sense of and practice each of the skills necessary to build competencies in regulation. This in turn provides the growth and development for learners to blossom into their regulation abilities.

APPLY YOUR LEARNING

Get Started!

1. Use the Leader Reflection Activity: Foundational Planning sheet to begin thinking about implementation. How will you build buy-in? Consider who will be leaders and who are other supportive adults to connect with to reinforce learning across settings. Also, include a plan to access the necessary resources for implementation.

2. Use the Leader Reflection Activity: Concept Planning and Progress sheet to explore and prepare for Concept 1 in *The Zones of Regulation Digital Curriculum*.

Zones Connection:

If you haven't yet subscribed to *The Zones of Regulation® Digital Curriculum*, follow the instructions provided in the back of the book to gain your free, 6-month access to Concept 1.

For full subscription information, please visit: https://zonesofregulation.com/explore-and-purchase-the-zones-products/

LEADER REFLECTION ACTIVITY: CHAPTER 4

CONCEPT PLANNER
CONCEPT 1

DIRECTIONS: Refer to "Concept 1: What Is Regulation?" in *The Zones of Regulation® Digital Curriculum*. Use this planner to help orient and prepare you for instruction. This checklist may be used to prepare for any concept within the curriculum.

Concept	
Date Range	
# of Sessions	
Resources to Print	☐ Group Activity: _____ ☐ Geared Activity(ies): _____ ☐ Check for Learning ☐ Bridge ☐ Zones Visual(s)
Other Materials	
Vocabulary	
Differentiation Notes	
Progress through Concept (check as complete)	☐ Hook ☐ Wrap-Up ☐ Core Lesson ☐ Check for Learning ☐ Group Activity ☐ Distribute Bridge ☐ Geared Activity

LEADER REFLECTION ACTIVITY: CHAPTER 4

FOUNDATIONAL PLANNING

DIRECTIONS: Fill in these foundational planning steps as they relate to your site.

YOUR "WHY"
How is The Zones of Regulation going to benefit your setting?

LEADERSHIP TEAM AND SUPPORTIVE ADULTS
Who should be involved?

RESOURCES NEEDED
Include training, curriculum subscription, books, supplementary resources

APPENDIX

APPENDIX: Chapter 1

SENSORY PREFERENCES AND LIFESTYLE: AVOIDING TO SEEKING SCALE

DIRECTIONS: Place an X indicating how each sense is perceived and provide examples underneath of ways sensory needs can be met through daily living activities and lifestyle.

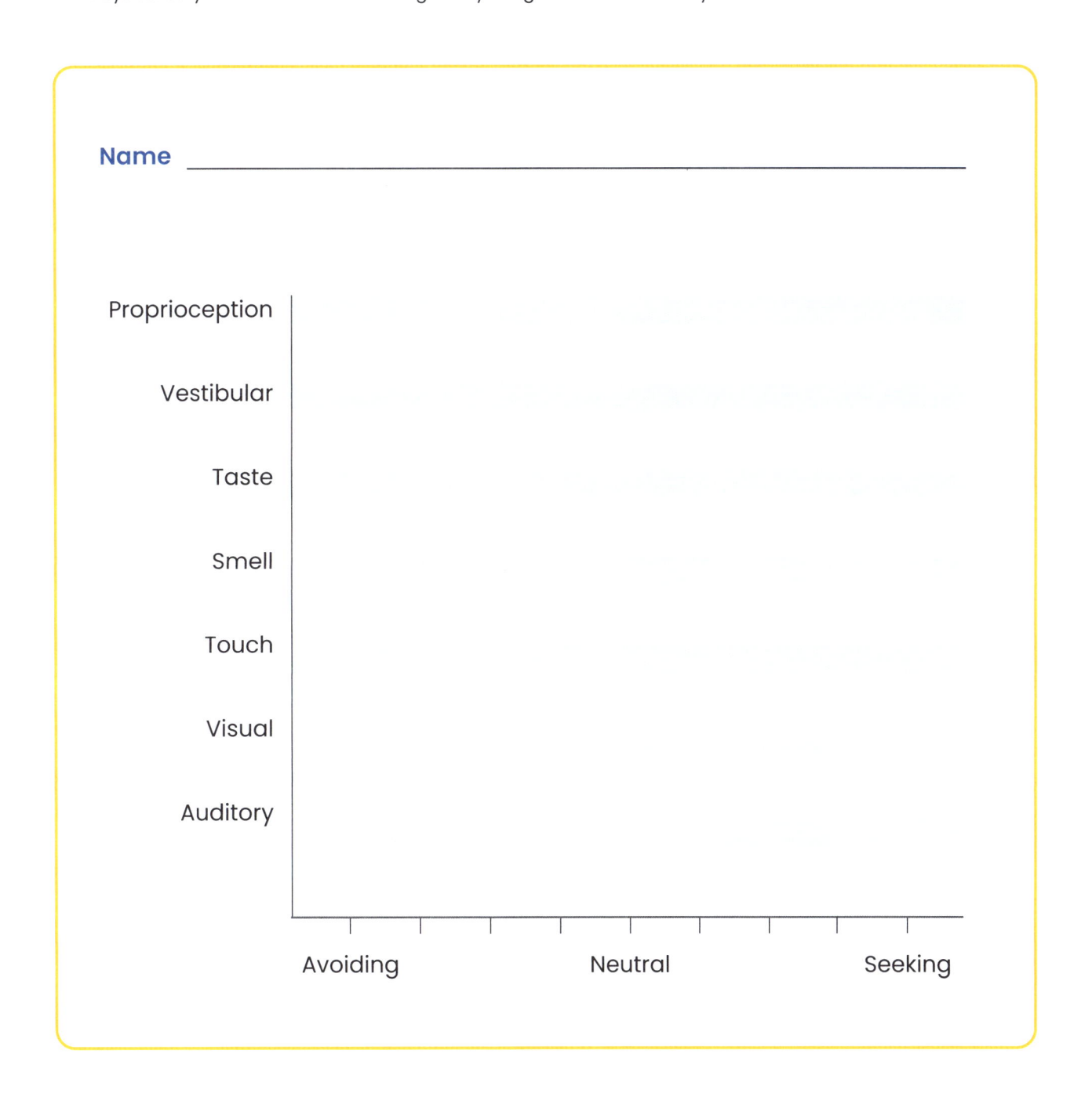

Name _____

Sense	Avoiding	Neutral	Seeking
Proprioception			
Vestibular			
Taste			
Smell			
Touch			
Visual			
Auditory			

©2024 The Zones of Regulation, Inc. All rights reserved. zonesofregulation.com

APPENDIX: Chapter 1

TOOLS FOR ASSESSING REGULATION COMPETENCIES

The list below contains several standardized and informal assessment measures and checklists that explore different aspects of regulation. Best practices to use prior to formal assessments include developing a relationship with a learner and their caregivers, identifying strengths and interests, and conducting observations across multiple settings to get to know a learner holistically. Additional considerations with any assessment or screener include age, trauma/ACEs, culture, race, language abilities, maturity, and intellectual functioning of the learner. Make sure to vet for potential biases such as cultural bias. This list is not all-inclusive and some tools that are listed may not be applicable to a specific learner's age and/or developmental level.

COMPREHENSIVE ASSESSMENT TOOLS

In order to deeply examine a learner's strengths, abilities, and unique needs, a combination of tools is needed for a comprehensive assessment of competencies and present levels of performance.

In school-based settings, a thorough examination of regulation in an individual is often divided among team members familiar with the learner, who have training in the assessment tools and can lend their expertise to the interpretation of results and direction of subsequent treatment/instruction. Given the dynamic nature of regulation, informal assessment tools, such as observation and interviews with the learner and caregivers, provide valuable insight.

Informal Qualitative Assessment Measures
- Assessment of Lagging Skills & Unsolved Problems (ALSUP) by Ross Greene; www.livesinthebalance.org/paperwork
- Interviews with caregivers, teacher(s), learner (when possible)
- Observation across settings with narrative data
- Zones Assessment tools; see Chapter 4 for more information

Executive Functioning Skills
- Behavior Rating Inventory of Executive Function® (BRIEF®) by Gerard A. Gioia; PhD; Peter K. Isquith, PhD; Steven C. Guy, PhD; and Lauren Kenworthy, PhD

Sensory Processing
- Sensory Processing Measure™ (SPM™) by Diane Parham and Cheryl Ecker
- Comprehensive Assessment for Interceptive Awareness by Kelly Mahler

APPENDIX: Chapter 1

Volition and Motivation
- The Pediatric Volitional Questionnaire (PVQ) Version 2.1 by Semonti Basu, Ana Kafkes, Rebecca Schatz, Anne Kiraly, and Gary Kielhofner
- The Volitional Questionnaire (VQ) Version 4.1 by Carmen Gloria de las Heras, Rebecca Geist, Gary Kielhofner, and Yanling Li

Social Cognition and Learning
- Walker-McConnell Scale of Social Competence and School Adjustment (WMS) by H. M. Walker and S. R. McConnell
- Social Skills Rating Scale (SSRS) by Stephen N. Elliott and Frank M. Gresham
- Social Thinking Dynamic Assessment Protocol, as discussed in *Thinking About YOU Thinking About ME*, 2nd ed. (2007) by Michelle Garcia Winner

Language and Problem Solving
- TOPS3-E: Test of Problem Solving-3 Elementary by Linda Bowers, Rosemary Huisingh, and Carolyn LoGiudice

Self-Regulation/Emotional Regulation
- Behavior Assessment System for Children, 3rd ed. (BASC-3) by Cecil R. Reynolds and Randy W. Kamphaus
- SCERTS® Model by Barry Prizant et al.
- HELP® 3–6, 2nd ed. (Hawaii Early Learning Profile) by VORT Corp.

Adverse Childhood Experiences (ACEs)/Trauma
- The Pediatric ACEs and Related Life-events Screener (PEARLS) by Bay Area Research Consortium on Toxic Stress and Health (BARC)
- The NCTSN CANS Comprehensive—Trauma Version: A comprehensive information integration tool for children and adolescents exposed to traumatic events by National Center for Child Traumatic Stress

SCREENERS FOR SCHOOLWIDE/TIER 1

On a schoolwide level (Tier 1), schools and districts are increasingly using Social Emotional Learning Screeners as a means for identifying learners who may need targeted supports/interventions and assessing overall trends in learner skills and need areas. Examples of screeners used in this capacity include:

- SSIS SEL Screener by Frank M. Gresham and Stephen N. Elliot, Pearson Assessments
- Social Emotional Assets and Resilience Scales (SEARS) Screener by Kenneth W. Merrell
- Devereaux Student Strengths Assessment-Mini (DESSA-mini) by Aperture Education

For further information on schoolwide SEL Screeners, visit: https://www.pbis.org/resource/systematic-screening-tools-universal-behavior-screeners.

APPENDIX: Chapter 1

ZONES OF REGULATION DIGITAL CURRICULUM AND CASEL COMPETENCY CORRELATION CHART

Zones Concept	Self-Awareness	Self-Management	Social Awareness	Relationship Skills	Responsible Decision-Making
C1: What Is Regulation?	X				
C2: Introducing The Zones of Regulation	X	X			X
C3: All The Zones Are Okay	X	X	X		
C4: My Signals, My Zones	X				X
C5: The Zones Check-In	X	X	X	X	
C6: Situations that Trigger and Spark	X	X	X	X	X
C7: What Is a Regulation Tool?		X	X		X
C8: Building My Zones Toolbox	X	X	X	X	X
C9: Deciding to Regulate	X	X	X	X	X
C10: The Zones Pathway	X	X	X		X

For more information on CASEL SEL Competencies, see: casel.org.

©2024 The Zones of Regulation, Inc. All rights reserved. zonesofregulation.com

APPENDIX: Chapter 3

ZONES CHECK-IN CONSIDERATIONS

DOs

✓ **DO** model first by "owning your zone" and checking in with all of your Zones to establish a safe climate that values all feelings.

✓ **DO** use a Zones Check-In as a non-judgmental communication strategy, reinforcing that ALL ZONES ARE OKAY.

✓ **DO** consider that checking in can feel hard for some learners due to self-awareness and their sense of safety and comfort in the situation.

✓ **DO** use observations and inquiry when checking in with learners. For example, "I see that your head is down, and you are yawning. What Zone are you in?"

✓ **DO** check-ins throughout the day to allow for self-reflection in all of The Zones.

DON'Ts

✗ **DON'T** make checking in one-sided just for learners. We all experience all of The Zones.

✗ **DON'T** connect a Zones Check-In to a compliance or punitive system. Remember: The Zones is not a behavior management system; there should be no rewards or punishments for being in any Zone.

✗ **DON'T** force someone to check in. It is crucial to respect the autonomy of each unique individual.

✗ **DON'T** label somebody's Zone for them. This can lead to misunderstanding and misinterpretation.

✗ **DON'T** only use Zones Check-Ins during challenging moments.

For more information on the Zones Check-In, see Chapter 2.
In addition, Concept 5 in *The Zones Digital Curriculum* is devoted to the Zones Check-In.

APPENDIX: Chapter 3

ZONES LANGUAGE

INSTEAD OF...	TRY...
"You need to calm down."	"Let's do a Zones Check-In."
"It's too loud in here."	"The noise in here is making ME feel like I'm in the Yellow Zone, and it's hard for me to think. I need to take a deep breath to manage my Zone."
"You need to take a break."	"How are you feeling? Should we try a tool?"
"You are losing points/getting clipped up on our level system."	"Let's check in with the Zones." If unable to identify a feeling or Zone, with permission, you might go on to say, "It looks like your body has a lot of energy and you are having a hard time focusing. Maybe you are feeling silly in the Yellow Zone. What's a tool that might help?"
"Don't worry about that."	"How can I help with this feeling?"
"You need to get back to the Green Zone."	"It is okay to be angry in the Red Zone **and** we need to have a safe body. Let's find a tool to help." (and show a visual of their Red Zone Toolbox choices)

APPENDIX: Chapter 3

THE ZONES CLIMATE RUBRIC

PURPOSE AND DIRECTIONS: This rubric can be used to reflect on the Essential Elements of the Zones Climate. It shows a continuum from basic implementation of Zones Climate strategies to inclusive, responsive, and agency-centered practices. Adapt this observational tool as needed to your setting's climate/culture, Zones leaders, and goals. Take into consideration that building the Zones Climate does not happen overnight, rather it is established over time as you move through *The Zones of Regulation® Digital Curriculum*. Each element notes when you may begin to implement these strategies during the course of instruction. The Zones Climate Rubric has two primary uses:

1. Reflection and Goal Setting:

Use this rubric to self-reflect on the integration of Zones Climate Elements; notice what is working well and set future goals. It could also be used to spark discussion within a professional learning community.

2. Walk-through:

This rubric may also be used within school (or similar) settings for a climate "walk-through." Select one element at a time as a "look-for," and time the walk-through to follow instruction of related concepts. For example, conduct a walk-through looking for Zones Visuals, allowing time for all leaders to teach "Concept 2: Introducing The Zones of Regulation." Use the data to celebrate successes, identify goals to work toward, and keep track of progress toward implementation goals.

---

0 = Not Yet (Insufficient)
Not in place, misuse

1 = Proficient
Basic elements

2 = Exemplary
Inclusive, learner agency IN ADDITION to basic elements

---

1. Provide Direct Instruction and Practice Opportunities

Dedicated time, practice, and reinforcement is provided for *The Zones of Regulation® Digital Curriculum* concepts, including connecting with supportive adults such as caregivers, teachers, therapists, support staff, etc. for carryover.

• No evidence yet of Zones instruction. • Visuals are posted/used without direct instruction of *The Zones Digital Curriculum*. • No time is set aside or dedicated to direct instruction.	• Direct instruction and practice is provided on a regular basis. • Instruction follows the scope and sequence of *The Zones Digital Curriculum*. • Zones concepts are reinforced in group discussions. • The Zones Bridge is shared with supportive adults (caregivers, therapists, teachers, etc.) for every concept taught.	All in proficient, and: • Zones instruction and pacing are adapted to best meet the needs of learners. • Zones concepts are reinforced continuously in large and small groups, individual conversations, and teachable moments. • Zones concepts are woven into academic content. • Sustained contact exists between supportive adults (caregivers, therapists, teachers, etc.) regarding concepts and strategies taught to generalize across settings.

©2024 The Zones of Regulation, Inc. All rights reserved. zonesofregulation.com

APPENDIX: Chapter 3

0 = Not Yet (Insufficient) Not in place, misuse	1 = Proficient Basic elements	2 = Exemplary Inclusive, learner agency IN ADDITION to basic elements

2. Post Zones Visuals
Zones posters and visuals are accessible for all to reference. *NOTE: This is not to be expected until **Concept 2** is taught in *The Zones Digital Curriculum*.

• Zones Visuals not yet present. • Visuals are placed in an area that cannot be easily seen/referenced by leaders or learners. • Clip chart/behavior management system with Zones colors is present, which misrepresents/undermines The Zones framework.	• Zones Visuals are posted. • Visuals are in a location that is easily referenced by leaders and learners. • Visuals are engaging for learners.	All in proficient, and: • Visuals are created in collaboration with learners. • Visuals are culturally and linguistically relevant, age appropriate, and reflective of learners. • Visuals incorporate accessible vocabulary and visual imagery. • Learners independently reference Zones Visuals and/or use them for non-verbal communication. • Visuals are referenced in conversations, discussions, and teachable moments.

3. Offer Zones Check-Ins
Learners and leaders have a system for noticing and communicating their Zone. Systems will vary according to the learner population. Remember, we never force others to check in but can provide alternative ways for them to communicate if/when ready. *NOTE: This is not to be expected until **Concept 5** is taught in *The Zones Digital Curriculum*.

• The Zones check-in system is not yet present. • The check-in system is used incorrectly to monitor learner behavior. • The check-in system is used punitively (i.e., earning or losing points depending on Zone). • The check-in system exists but is not used often.	• The Zones Check-In system provides a non-verbal way to communicate one's Zone. • The check-in system is used at a scheduled time, such as when entering the setting. • Leaders participate in the check-in system and share as appropriate.	All in proficient, and: • Learners have agency to check in at both scheduled times *and* when they feel the need. • Staff model "owning your Zone" by publicly checking in, verbally and with the system. • Non-verbal check-in system is culturally and linguistically relevant, age appropriate, and reflective of learner population. • Learners show comfort with check-in system. • The check-in system is inclusive and accessible for all learners in the setting.

©2024 The Zones of Regulation, Inc. All rights reserved. zonesofregulation.com

APPENDIX: Chapter 3

0 = Not Yet (Insufficient) Not in place, misuse	1 = Proficient Basic elements	2 = Exemplary Inclusive, learner agency IN ADDITION to basic elements

4. Easy Access to Regulation Tools
Learners and leaders have access and opportunities to use regulation tools within their setting. This can look like a "regulation station" of some type, basket of tools, or having toolbox visuals to remind learners of options. In the Zones Climate, using tools is the norm, not the exception. *NOTE: This is not to be expected until Concepts 7 and 8 are taught from *The Zones Digital Curriculum*.

• Access to regulation tools not yet present. • Tools are only taught to and used by select learners. • Learners need to leave their learning environment to access tools. • Regulation tools are provided without any instruction, modeling, or practice. • No routines or expectations are set or maintained for use of tools (such as how to transition in and out of a regulation space). • Use of a regulation area (or a tool) is commanded as a punitive measure or with a negative association.	• All learners are taught how to use regulation tools. • A few regulation tools are referenced/provided. • Leaders prompt learners to use the regulation tools in a proactive manner. • A regulation area and/or a community toolbox is posted. • Learners are given opportunities to practice using tools when regulated. • Expectations around tool use are taught (i.e., use as intended, transition after, time adherence, etc.).	All in proficient, and: • Learners show comfort with using regulation tools. • A variety of tools/strategies is available, including movement-based tools, sensory tools, mindfulness/breathing strategies, fidgets, cognitive strategies, etc. • Learners show agency and independence as they self-select to use their tools and the Regulation Station. • Learners have individualized toolboxes, and a community toolbox with ideas is posted. • Leaders model using tools throughout the day and have their own toolbox visible for reference. • Learners use tools responsibly (i.e., use as intended, transition after, time adherence, etc.).

©2024 The Zones of Regulation, Inc. All rights reserved. zonesofregulation.com

APPENDIX: Chapter 3

0 = Not Yet (Insufficient) Not in place, misuse	1 = Proficient Basic elements	2 = Exemplary Inclusive, learner agency IN ADDITION to basic elements

5. Use Zones Language

Leaders and learners use Zones terminology and language that promote regulation and wellness throughout the day. Examples: *"I'm feeling tired in the Blue Zone. Can anyone help me think of a tool to care for my Zone?" "I notice your body is moving really quickly. What Zone are you in?" "What tool did that character use to manage their Zone?"* *NOTE: This is not expected until learners are given adequate time to explore and practice introductory Zones concepts.

• Zones-friendly language is not observed. • Leaders describe Zones based on outward behavior rather than internal state. • Leaders assign Zones to learners rather than asking or offering observations. • Misuse of The Zones framework, such as indicating that the Red Zone is the bad Zone or telling learners they need to get back to the Green Zone.	• Zones language is used during specific Zones lessons. • Zones language used in assigned SEL time such as in morning meeting, etc. • Zones language is being used in individual conversations with learners. • Leaders "own their Zone" and talk about their own feelings. • Zones language is just used by those providing instruction.	All in proficient, and: • Zones language is used throughout the day. • All adults in a setting are using Zones as common language. • Learners use Zones language both with and without prompting/framing. • Zones language and concepts are used in group discussions. • Leaders pair verbal with visual cues when referencing Zones. • References to Zones concepts are observed during academic instruction, such as within discussions about characters, current and historical events, etc.

©2024 The Zones of Regulation, Inc. All rights reserved. zonesofregulation.com

APPENDIX: Chapter 4

CONCEPT PLANNER

Concept

Date Range

# of Sessions

Resources to Print
- ☐ Group Activity:
- ☐ Geared Activity(ies):

☐ Group Activity:
☐ Geared Activity(ies):

☐ Group Activity:
☐ Geared Activity(ies):

☐ Check for Learning
☐ Bridge
☐ Zones Visual(s)

☐ Check for Learning
☐ Bridge
☐ Zones Visual(s)

☐ Check for Learning
☐ Bridge
☐ Zones Visual(s)

Other Materials

Vocabulary

Differentiation Notes

Progress through Concept (check as complete)
- ☐ Hook
- ☐ Core Lesson
- ☐ Group Activity
- ☐ Geared Activity
- ☐ Wrap-Up
- ☐ Check for Learning
- ☐ Distribute Bridge

- ☐ Hook
- ☐ Core Lesson
- ☐ Group Activity
- ☐ Geared Activity
- ☐ Wrap-Up
- ☐ Check for Learning
- ☐ Distribute Bridge

- ☐ Hook
- ☐ Core Lesson
- ☐ Group Activity
- ☐ Geared Activity
- ☐ Wrap-Up
- ☐ Check for Learning
- ☐ Distribute Bridge

©2024 The Zones of Regulation, Inc. All rights reserved. zonesofregulation.com

APPENDIX: Chapter 4

SAMPLE INDIVIDUALIZED REGULATION GOALS

These are goal and objective ideas that can be adapted for Individualized Education Plans (IEPs), interventions, and treatment plans to accompany Zones of Regulation instruction. Please collaborate with the learner, caregivers, teacher, and other supportive adults to develop and adapt them as appropriate for each unique learner and setting. Keep in mind that IEP goals should be specific, measurable, achievable, relevant, and time-bound (SMART).

- [Learner] will increase emotional vocabulary as demonstrated by labeling emotions _____, _____, and _____ in self and others in ____ out of ____ opportunities.

- [Learner] will increase emotional vocabulary from ____ to ____ common feelings/emotions in ____ out of ____ opportunities.

- Given a check-in system and routine (such as a Zones Check-In), [Learner] will verbally or non-verbally identify and/or communicate their feelings using emotional vocabulary or naming system (Zone) in ____ out of ____ opportunities.

- [Learner] will name one or more body signals they experience in relation to at least four emotions (Zones) in ____ out of ____ opportunities.

- Given a situation, [Learner] can identify or explain at least two different perspectives of how others may feel in ____ out of ____ opportunities.

- [Learner] will identify at least ____ situations that are "triggers" or cause them to have uncomfortable or less regulated feelings in ____ out of ____ opportunities.

- [Learner] will demonstrate at least ____ regulation tools or strategies that they can use to manage their feelings in ____ out of ____ opportunities.

- [Learner] will identify at least ____ tools they find calming (Yellow Zone and Red Zone tools), ____ tools that help support their well-being (Green Zone tools), and ____ tools that help them re-energize (Blue Zone tools) in ____ out of ____ opportunities.

- Given visual/verbal prompting and access to regulation tools (Zones Toolbox), [Learner] will select and use a tool/strategy to regulate in a real-time situation in ____ out of ____ opportunities.

- [Learner] will identify at least one situation within the day/week in which they would have benefited from using a regulation tool in ____ out of ____ opportunities.

- [Learner] is able to pause or delay an impulse to think through options when faced with a problem or stressor in ____ out of ____ opportunities.

- Given a problem or triggering situation, [Learner] can identify and reflect on three or more options including using a regulation tool vs. not using a regulation tool in ____ out of ____ opportunities.

- [Learner] will identify at least one situation within the day/week in which they regulated successfully in ____ out of ____ opportunities.

- [Learner] can reflect on real-time situations when they did regulate vs. did not regulate and the impact it had on their outcomes and goals in ____ out of ____ opportunities.

APPENDIX: Chapter 4

ZONES IN THE HOME

Using The Zones of Regulation in home and residential settings can be beneficial for both learners and the grown-ups who support them. The concepts found in *The Zones of Regulation Digital Curriculum* can be directly taught within a family unit or caregivers can support learners by creating a Zones Climate at home. In addition to the tips below, explore the Zones Bridge activities within the Digital Curriculum to help extend regulation skills into the home.

Here are some tips to support using The Zones in a home setting:

- Create a visual of the four Zones for the home. You may choose to incorporate pictures of family members (and pets) modeling various feelings for each Zone. (Concept 2)

- Use Zones Check-Ins on a regular basis to connect as a family. This can look like each family member having their name on a sticky note or clothespin and using the visual of the four Zones to check in by moving their sticky note or clothespin throughout the day. (Concept 5)

- Model using the visuals and the Zones language with all family members.

- When reading books or watching movies together, infuse Zones language into reflections on the characters' feelings, behaviors, and/or tools as they manage their Zones.

- Have a family discussion around tools for each Zone, putting together a family Zones Toolbox that can be displayed visually. In addition, put together a collection of objects that work as tools in a designated space for easy access by all. (Concepts 7 and 8)

- Explore tools that a young learner gravitates to in the home and community to personalize the learner's toolbox. Take pictures of the tools that a learner finds effective and add them to their Zones Toolbox visual. (Concepts 7 and 8)

- Try out a Tool of the Week by choosing a regulation tool or strategy to try each week as a family. Some examples are journaling, listening to music, going for a nature walk, eating a healthy snack, and taking screen breaks. Collect your favorite tools in a family Zones Toolbox. Check out our *Tools to Try Cards for Kids* and *Tools to Try Cards for Tweens & Teens* for ready-to-go tool ideas. (Concept 8)

- Build a comfort corner or regulation station by creating a place (or two) for kids and family members to go when they want to regulate. Choose a space that's comfortable and quiet, and include items such as stuffed animals, coloring books, fidgets, and books. Practice using your designated space a few times together. Caregivers can model by using it themselves when they need a break.

- Tools can be reviewed and reinforced by making a book, video, or slideshow of the learner using their tools that the family can reference frequently with the learner when they are in a calm state.

- The family can work together to use tools, giving each other Tool Tickets and working together to accumulate a set amount to earn a special reward they decide on. (Concept 10)

- *The Zones of Regulation Storybook Set*, Zones apps, *Tools to Try* card decks, and *Navigating The Zones* game can be used to reinforce and explore Zones concepts.

- Family Game Night with games like UNO, Sorry!, and Twister can easily be turned into opportunities to practice and reinforce The Zones. Take turns naming an emotion or experience for each red-, yellow-, green-, or blue-colored Zone during game play.

APPENDIX: Chapter 4

MTSS/PBIS AND ZONES OF REGULATION CROSSWALK

	Description	Zones of Regulation Instruction/ Interventions at Each Tier
TIER 1	MTSS: Core Programming PBIS: Universal Prevention Schoolwide programming and direct instruction in social, emotional, and behavioral competencies is provided for all learners. Instruction is proactive, preventive, and universal.	• Zones concepts are taught schoolwide in general education classrooms as positive, proactive instruction to promote regulation, wellness, and inclusion. • Zones of Regulation is used as a common language within the building by all staff and learners, including restorative and problem-solving discussions. • Zones Visuals are found throughout the building. • All learners and leaders are encouraged to participate in Zones Check-Ins as part of their daily routines. • A variety of regulation tools is accessible for both learners and leaders to use across settings. • Caregivers/families provide input and are provided information on The Zones of Regulation framework and how to carry over practices in the home/community.
TIER 2	MTSS: Supplemental Interventions PBIS: Targeted Prevention Interventions are targeted toward learners identified as "at-risk" or needing additional supplement to Tier 1 instruction. This may consist of small group, and/or targeted behavioral or mental health supports.	• Learners with like social, emotional, and/or behavioral goals are grouped for more frequent and targeted instruction of Zones of Regulation concepts. • Differentiated/adapted instruction of Zones content is provided, using the curriculum differentiation features and guidance, to match strengths, development, goals, and needs. • More opportunities to practice and apply Zones concepts are embedded throughout the day. • Increased access to individualized tools/strategies is provided. • Increased positive reinforcement around identifying feelings/ Zones and using tools to regulate is provided. • Collaboration between home, community settings, and school is provided for consistent use of Zones of Regulation programming across settings.
TIER 3	MTSS: Intensive Intervention PBIS: Intensive, Individualized Prevention Intensified and individualized interventions and "wrap around" support is provided for learners needing additional supplements to both Tier 1 and Tier 2 supports.	• Individualized Zones of Regulation instruction and visual supports tailored to learner's strengths, development, and interests are provided. • More frequent exposure and/or 1:1 instruction and practice around Zones of Regulation concepts is provided. • Trained staff offer additional co-regulation supports. • Learners receive increased access to individualized tools/ strategies, as well as frequent practice in using tools when in a calm state. • Increased positive reinforcement around identifying feelings/ Zones and using tools to regulate is provided. • Increased consultation between home, school, and outside providers such as therapists is provided. • Individualized positive behavior support plans are developed to guide staff in supporting learner's regulation and well-being.

*NOTE that learners receiving special education services have access to instructional support in any tiers that apply to their unique skills, needs, and goals.

Resources: Multi-Level Prevention System | Center on Multi-Tiered Systems of Support (mtss4success.org) Center on PBIS (pbis.org)

©2024 The Zones of Regulation, Inc. All rights reserved. zonesofregulation.com

APPENDIX: Chapter 4

REGULATION SELF-REFLECTION

Purpose: This is a self-assessment for individual learners that can be administered before and after implementation of *The Zones of Regulation® Digital Curriculum* to determine progress and guide instruction. Each item aligns to core concepts and practices taught in the curriculum as shown in the Concept Correlation Chart on this page. Use this tool to evaluate how well individual learners, as well as the whole group, have learned key Zones concepts and practices. When using as a whole group evaluation tool, compare the average score for the group before implementing the curriculum to the average score after implementation to evaluate growth. You can also look for patterns within individual items to guide instruction.

Directions: Questions may be read independently, read aloud to a group, or asked 1-on-1 with learners. Learners may answer questions independently or with the help of an adult scribe. Have learners select one answer choice for each item. Share definitions of unfamiliar words with learners as needed.

IF SCORING THIS ASSESSMENT:

Example:

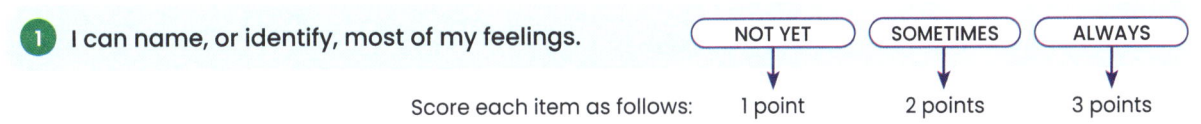

1 I can name, or identify, most of my feelings.   NOT YET   SOMETIMES   ALWAYS

Score each item as follows: 1 point   2 points   3 points

CONCEPT CORRELATION CHART

Item Number	Correlating Concept(s)
1	Concept 2
2	Concept 3
3	Concept 4
4	Concept 5
5	Concept 5
6	Concept 6
7	Concepts 7–8
8	Concepts 7–8
9	Concepts 7–8
10	Concept 8
11	Concept 9
12	Concept 10

©2024 The Zones of Regulation, Inc. All rights reserved. zonesofregulation.com

APPENDIX: Chapter 4

REGULATION SELF-REFLECTION

Learner Name: _____

Directions: Mark your choice for each statement.

#	Statement			
1	I can name, or identify, most of my feelings.	NOT YET	SOMETIMES	ALWAYS
2	I notice how people around me are feeling.	NOT YET	SOMETIMES	ALWAYS
3	I notice the body signals or sensations that come with my emotions (such as a fast heartbeat).	NOT YET	SOMETIMES	ALWAYS
4	I am comfortable sharing my feelings with others.	NOT YET	SOMETIMES	ALWAYS
5	I notice when my feelings change during the day.	NOT YET	SOMETIMES	ALWAYS
6	I can name things that often bother me or make me feel uncomfortable (such as loud noises, changes in schedule, cutting in line).	NOT YET	SOMETIMES	ALWAYS
7	I know 2–3 tools or strategies I can use to calm down and feel more in control.	NOT YET	SOMETIMES	ALWAYS
8	I know 2–3 tools or strategies I can use to feel more awake, focused, or energetic.	NOT YET	SOMETIMES	ALWAYS
9	I know 2–3 tools or strategies I can use to keep feeling healthy and comfortable throughout the day.	NOT YET	SOMETIMES	ALWAYS
10	I am willing to try and practice new tools.	NOT YET	SOMETIMES	ALWAYS
11	I can pause and think about my choices when I'm having a problem.	NOT YET	SOMETIMES	ALWAYS
12	I use tools or strategies in the moment to help me with my feelings and behavior.	NOT YET	SOMETIMES	ALWAYS

DONE

For Teacher Only

Add the totals for each column and divide by 12.

SCORE _____

_____ (total number of tallies above) x 1 = _____

_____ (total number of tallies above) x 2 = _____

_____ (total number of tallies above) x 3 = _____

THE ZONES OF REGULATION

©2024 The Zones of Regulation, Inc. All rights reserved. zonesofregulation.com

APPENDIX: Chapter 4

LEARNING TARGET RUBRIC

PURPOSE AND DIRECTIONS: This tool assists you in monitoring and tracking a learner's progress, and in planning and pacing instruction of *The Zones of Regulation® Digital Curriculum*. Use observations, questions, and concept activities, in addition to the Check for Learning to gauge and rate a learner's understanding of the learning targets on the rubric.

NOTE: The goal of The Zones of Regulation is growth along each learner's developmental continuum, not "mastery" of each learning target; this will look different for each learner. Therefore, it's important to measure progress in terms of a learner's individual growth, rather than how they compare to a "norm" or age level.

0	1	2	3	4	5
No grasp of concept or targets taught. Can't demonstrate with maximal support.	Emerging awareness of concept. May be able to point out or provide examples in others to demonstrate understanding, but unable to demonstrate concept with maximal support or provide personal examples of concept.	Emerging awareness of concept. Learner can point out and provide personal meaningful examples of concept and can demonstrate by applying concept with maximum to moderate adult support/cueing.	Solid understanding of concept and can demonstrate by applying concept with moderate to minimal adult support and cueing.	Solid understanding of concept and can demonstrate by applying concept with minimal to no adult support and cueing.	Learner can demonstrate knowledge of the concept independently during real-time events. Learner can teach and model concept to others.

IF YOU RATE A LEARNER AT 0

Use adaptation suggestions within the Concept Guide, as well as Geared Activities, to further practice and reinforce this skill. If a learner's understanding remains at a 0 over time, consider the appropriateness of the curriculum for this learner.

IF YOU RATE A LEARNER AT A 1 OR 2

Spend more time teaching and give the learner opportunities to apply this concept before moving on to the next one. Explore concepts using alternative adaptation suggestions, Geared Activities, modeling media such as literature and video, and any additional outside resources that provide learner with further opportunity to explore content. Consider accessibility and any modifications that may be warranted.

IF YOU RATE A LEARNER AT A 3, 4, OR 5

Continue to use the concept in context and apply in real time during teachable moments as they arise. Increase learner agency, enabling them to explore, communicate, and apply concepts their own way. Use your judgment to determine if the learner is ready to move on to a new concept or explore further. Spiral back to concepts over time, encouraging learner to build a deeper understanding.

©2024 The Zones of Regulation, Inc. All rights reserved. zonesofregulation.com

APPENDIX: Chapter 4

LEARNING TARGET RUBRIC

Learner Name: _____

Zones Leader Name: _____   Instructional Date or Period: _____

Concept and Learning Target	Q1	Q2	Q3	Q4	Notes
C1: I can use the word "regulate" in a sentence.					
I can describe one or more ways a person may regulate themselves.					
C2: I can name and describe the four Zones of Regulation.					
I can sort, or categorize, feelings into the four Zones of Regulation.					
C3: I can connect my feelings and Zones with real-life situations.					
I can give an example of how people have different feelings and perspectives in a situation.					
C4: I can name at least one body signal I feel when I am in each Zone.					
I can explain how body signals, Zones, and emotions are all connected.					
C5: I can pause and do a Zones Check-In on my own or with others.					
With practice, I can check in when I am in each of the Zones: Red, Yellow, Green, Blue.					

©2024 The Zones of Regulation, Inc. All rights reserved. zonesofregulation.com

APPENDIX: Chapter 4

LEARNING TARGET RUBRIC

Concept and Learning Target	Q1	Q2	Q3	Q4	Notes
C6: I can notice and describe the situation around me (when, where, what, who).					
I can name at least two of my triggers and two of my sparks.					
C7: I can identify common regulation tools around me.					
I can use The Zones of Regulation to categorize regulation tools.					
C8: I can reflect on how a tool helps me regulate.					
I can share a helpful tool from each Zone in my toolbox.					
C9: I can pause to think about my options and goals before acting.					
I can decide if using a regulation tool will help in a situation.					
C10: I can use the Zones Pathway in real-time situations.					
Using the Zones Pathway, I can reflect on how my regulation is working for me.					

©2024 The Zones of Regulation, Inc. All rights reserved. zonesofregulation.com

145

APPENDIX: Chapter 4

OBSERVING REGULATION COMPETENCIES

Purpose: Use this tool to evaluate learners' competencies in the key concepts taught in *The Zones of Regulation Digital Curriculum*. Each item correlates to core concepts and practices taught in the curriculum as shown in the Concept Correlation Chart® on this page. You may choose to administer this inventory before and after intervention using *The Zones Digital Curriculum* or midway through as a way to monitor progress. This inventory does not have a scoring component; rather, results may be used to make decisions regarding progress of individuals or groups of learners and to guide instruction. You can also look for patterns within individual items to guide group instruction.

Directions: This assessment tool should be completed by an adult who has an established positive relationship with the learner. Reflect on how the individual learner has exhibited each competency over a period of a couple of weeks, depending on the frequency of interaction/observation. If possible, use data such as learner anecdotal notes as a reference when completing this tool and consider completing it with other adults who regularly work with the learner. You may also prompt learners directly to reflect on specific question items, such as "How does your body feel when you're in the Blue Zone?"

CONCEPT CORRELATION CHART

Item Number	Correlating Concept(s)
1	Concept 2
2	Concept 3
3	Concept 3
4	Concept 4
5	Concept 5
6	Concept 5
7	Concept 6
8	Concepts 7–8
9	Concepts 7–8
10	Concepts 7–8
11	Concept 8
12	Concepts 9–10
13	Concept 10
14	Concept 10
15	Concepts 9–10

©2024 The Zones of Regulation, Inc. All rights reserved. zonesofregulation.com

APPENDIX: Chapter 4

OBSERVING REGULATION COMPETENCIES

Learner Name: _____

Date Administered: _____

Administered by: _____

		1 Not Yet	2 Rarely	3 Sometimes	4 Often	5 Always
1	Learner can identify a range of their emotions/feelings.					
2	Learner can predict how they might feel in a variety of situations (such as a class celebration, or when someone calls them a name).					
3	Learner notices and identifies others' feelings and perspectives.					
4	Learner can identify the body signals/sensations associated with different feelings (such as heart racing when upset, etc.).					
5	Learner communicates feelings with supportive adults.					
6	Learner is aware of how their feelings and energy levels fluctuate throughout the day.					
7	Learner can identify situations/conditions that are triggers or cause them to feel less regulated (such as loud noises, changes in schedule, cutting in line, etc.).					
8	Learner can identify and demonstrate a variety of regulation tools/strategies to help them calm down and feel in control (Yellow and Red Zone tools).					
9	Learner can identify and demonstrate a variety of regulation tools/strategies to help them feel more awake, focused, or energized (Blue Zone tools).					
10	Learner can identify and demonstrate a variety of regulation tools/strategies that can help them maintain their health, wellness, and comfort (Green Zone tools).					
11	Learner willingly practices and reflects on new regulation tools.					
12	Learner is able to delay an impulse in order to think through options when facing a problem or stressor.					
13	With prompting or support, learner uses tools/strategies to regulate.					
14	Learner can independently use tools/strategies to regulate.					
15	Learner can connect regulating their feelings and behaviors with positive outcomes, such as achieving goals.					

THE ZONES OF REGULATION

©2024 The Zones of Regulation, Inc. All rights reserved. zonesofregulation.com

APPENDIX: Chapter 4

DIGITAL CURRICULUM IMPLEMENTATION & FIDELITY CHECKLIST

Name:_____ Date:_____ Setting (circle one): Whole class | Small group | Individual
Concept # Observed: _____

Use Part A and Part B to score implementation fidelity on *The Zones of Regulation® Digital Curriculum*; scoring details at the bottom. NOTE: Deep knowledge of The Zones of Regulation framework and Digital Curriculum are essential to observing for program fidelity.

PART A: OBSERVATION FORM	NOT EVIDENT: 0	SOMEWHAT EVIDENT: 1	MOSTLY EVIDENT: 2	COMPLETELY EVIDENT: 3
QUALITY				
Leader facilitates active engagement and participation from learners, using strategies presented in the Concept Guide.				
Most learners are engaged in instruction (e.g., asking/answering questions, Pair & Share, participating in digital and hands-on activities).				
Leader models the use of Zones language and vocabulary throughout instruction.				
Leader adapts instruction for learners (development, age, neurology, culture, language, and life experiences). Circle adaptation(s) observed.				
Leader uses strategies such as questioning and observation throughout instruction (e.g., learner work, Pair & Share, discussions) to evaluate learner understanding.				
Leader normalizes a wide range of feelings in their setting (i.e., all feelings and Zones are okay).				
Leader co-regulates with learners using strategies (e.g., verbal and non-verbal Zones Check-Ins, prompting learners to use regulation tools, providing visual supports for communication, etc). Circle the co-regulation strategy(ies) observed.				
Leader has a Zones Check-In routine and system accessible to learners and supporting adults (after teaching Concept 5).				
Leader provides easy access to regulation tools and strategies and normalizes their use (after teaching Concepts 7, 8).				
ADHERENCE				
Leader is prepared to teach concept content: has prepared and reviewed instructional materials in advance of teaching this concept (e.g., printable handouts, Zones Visuals, Bridge, etc.).				
Leader posts relevant Zones Visuals in areas visible to learners.				

PART B: INTERVIEW — How many concepts in Digital Curriculum have you taught? _____	NEVER: 0	RARELY: 1	OFTEN: 2	ALWAYS: 3
ADHERENCE				
Do you deliver instructional components in the recommended sequence (Hook, Core Lesson, Group Activity, Geared Activity, Wrap-Up)?				
Do you administer the Check for Learning (formative assessment) to learners?				
Do you distribute the Zones Bridge to family/caregivers and/or relevant partners?				
Do you use the data from the Check for Learning, or alternative provided in each Concept Guide, to evaluate learner understanding and inform further instruction?				
EXPOSURE				
Do you dedicate at least **40 minutes per week** to direct instruction of new Zones concepts and/or to reinforce concepts previously taught? *Note: The 40 minutes can be spread over the course of the week.*				
Do you reinforce Zones Concepts and apply them outside of direct instruction of the Zones curriculum?				
Are you teaching the concepts in *The Zones Digital Curriculum* in the sequence suggested?				

SCORING (54 TOTAL POINTS POSSIBLE)
High Fidelity = 43 points or more (> 80% +)
Moderate Fidelity (some improvement needed) = 32–42 points (60–79%)
Low Fidelity (significant improvement needed) = 31 points or less (<60%)

TOTAL PER CATEGORY

TOTAL SCORE

Teaching Pathways

Getting Into The Zones of Regulation orients you to the next evolution of the Zones of Regulation theory and methods.

It can be used 2 ways:

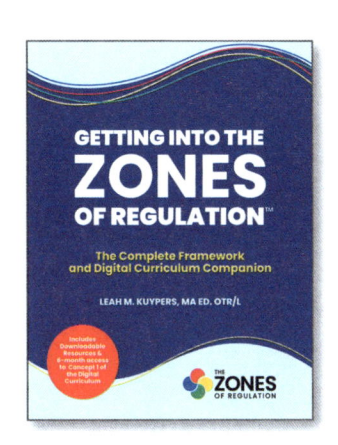

①

If you prefer digital, use it to prepare you to teach the concepts and lessons in *The Zones Digital Curriculum*. Learn more about the subscription-based curriculum at www.zonesofregulation.com.

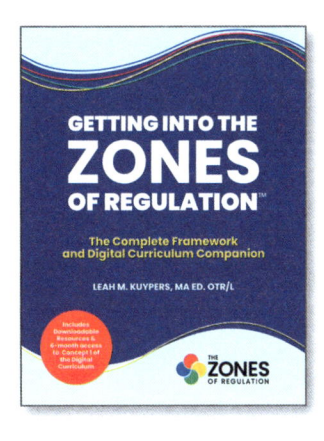

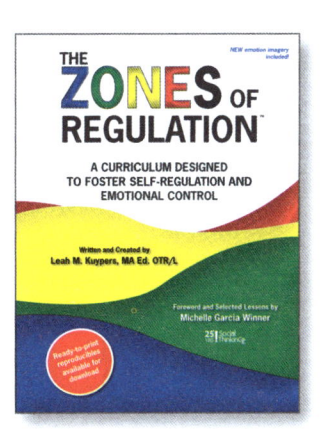

②

Or, if you prefer print, use this book to update your practices in combination with the lessons and handouts from the original *[The] Zones of Regulation* book.

Either way, see the details on the inside back cover to start your **6-month free access to Concept 1** to try out all the new interactive features of the Digital Curriculum.

Continue the learning with more Zones supplemental teaching materials

THE ZONES OF REGULATION

Award Winning Series for All Ages

All products available at www.socialthinking.com

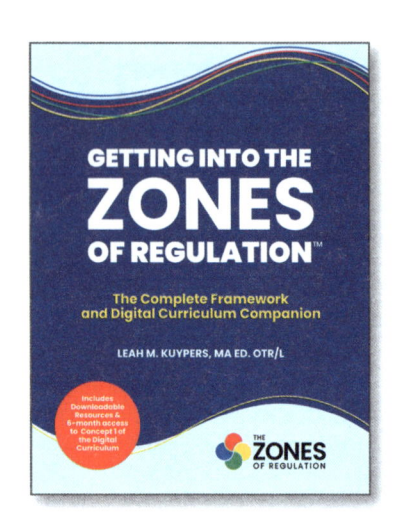

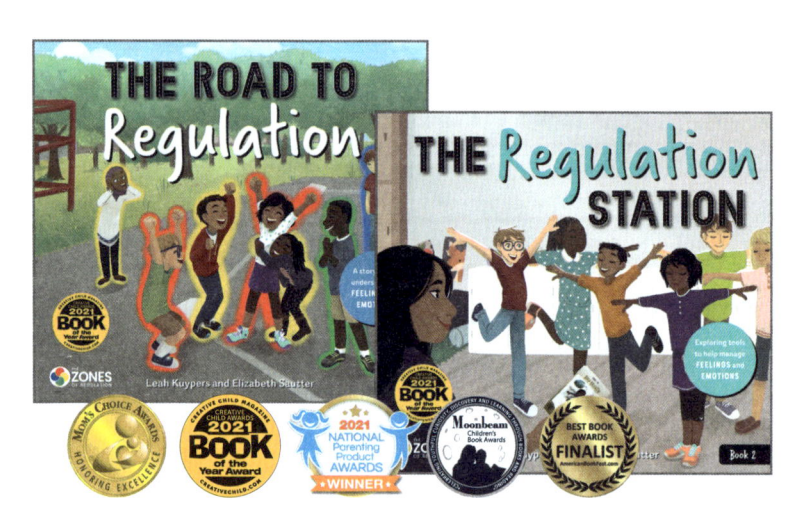

Books

Getting Into The Zones of Regulation

The Road to Regulation & The Regulation Station: Understanding and Managing Feelings & Emotions (2-storybook set)

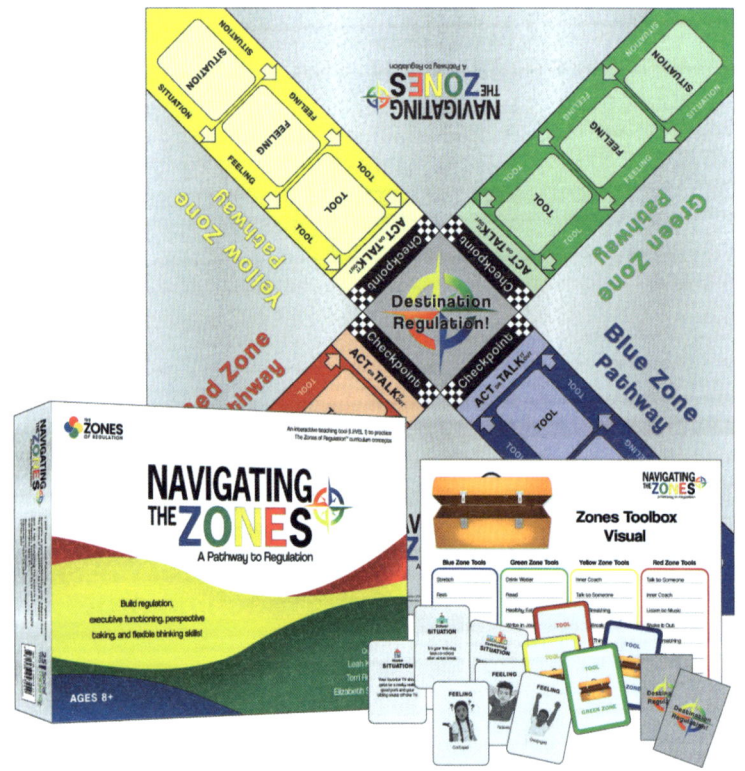

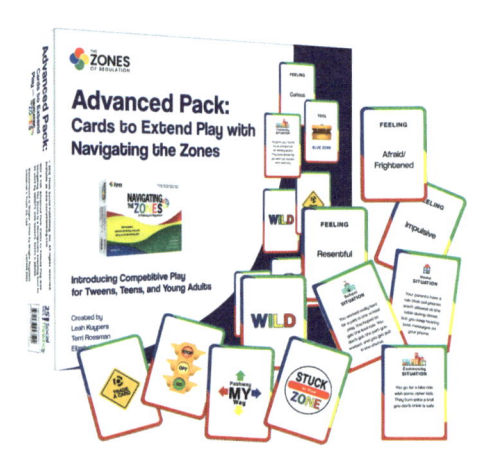

Games

Navigating The Zones

Advanced Pack

Card Decks

Tools to Try Cards for Kids

Tools to Try Cards for Tweens & Teens

Posters

The Zones of Regulation Digital Curriculum 5-Poster Set:
Zones Triggers & Sparks poster (dry-erase)
Zones Stop, Opt & Go poster (dry-erase)
Zones Check-In poster (dry-erase)
The Zones of Regulation Tools poster (dry-erase)
Zones Pathway poster

The Road to Regulation Poster

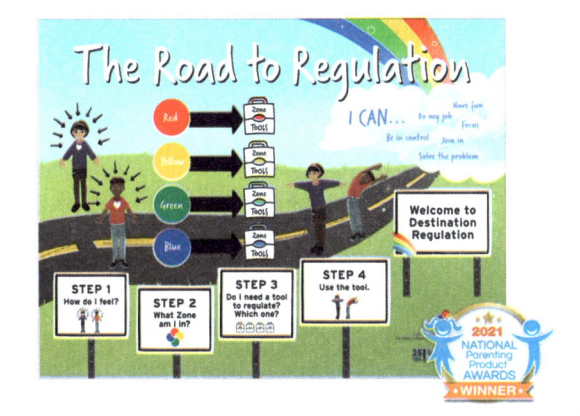

All products available at www.socialthinking.com

NOTES

NOTES

ABOUT THE AUTHOR

Leah Kuypers, MA Ed., OTR/L, is the creator of The Zones of Regulation, a framework designed to foster regulation. She is the author of *The Zones of Regulation® Digital Curriculum* (zonesofregulation.com, 2024) and the new companion print book *Getting Into The Zones of Regulation™: The Complete Framework and Digital Curriculum Companion* (Think Social Publishing, 2024). In addition, she is the author of two Zones of Regulation apps, as well as co-creator of *Navigating The Zones* and *Advanced Pack*, a game and it's expansion deck, the Zones storybook set, and *Tools to Try* card decks, all published by Think Social Publishing. Leah provides trainings and consultation to districts, professionals, and caregivers on regulation and social emotional learning and conducts workshops on The Zones of Regulation framework to groups around the world. Explore the *Digital Curriculum*, webinars, and trainings at the website, www.zonesofregulation.com. Leah resides in Minneapolis, Minnesota, with her husband, son, and daughter.